"*A Patchwork Heart* is a study that will help you enlarge your heart to contain more of God's love and compassion for others. It will help you see through God's eyes the people He has put into your life. What a change in perspective!"

—LINDA EVANS SHEPHERD, speaker;
author, *Teatime Stories for Women*;
founder, Advanced Writers and Speakers Association

"If you're hurting, if you're wondering why God hasn't changed your circumstances, if you're asking those 'why' questions of life, then this is the book for you! In *A Patchwork Heart*, Kim Moore and Pam Mellskog beautifully share their own journey to a patchwork heart and how they've discovered that there can be, and often is, a purpose for our suffering. You can't know Kim and Pam and not see that they know what it truly means to have the heart of Christ. I highly recommend their new book. It'll forever change how you look at those difficult places in life."

—MARTHA BOLTON, Emmy-nominated writer for Bob Hope;
author of 45 books and *The Cafeteria Lady*

DEEPENING YOUR LOVE FOR OTHERS
INCLUDES A TEN-WEEK BIBLE STUDY

Foreword by
CAROL KENT

A
Patchwork
HEART

KIM MOORE
& PAM MELLSKOG

NAVPRESS

BRINGING TRUTH TO LIFE
P.O. Box 35001, Colorado Springs, Colorado 80935

OUR GUARANTEE TO YOU

We believe so strongly in the message of our books that we are making this quality guarantee to you. If for any reason you are disappointed with the content of this book, return the title page to us with your name and address and we will refund to you the list price of the book. To help us serve you better, please briefly describe why you were disappointed. Mail your refund request to: NavPress, P.O. Box 35002, Colorado Springs, CO 80935.

The Navigators is an international Christian organization. Our mission is to reach, disciple, and equip people to know Christ and to make Him known through successive generations. We envision multitudes of diverse people in the United States and every other nation who have a passionate love for Christ, live a lifestyle of sharing Christ's love, and multiply spiritual laborers among those without Christ.

NavPress is the publishing ministry of The Navigators. NavPress publications help believers learn biblical truth and apply what they learn to their lives and ministries. Our mission is to stimulate spiritual formation among our readers.

Library of Congress Catalog Card Number: 2002002123
ISBN 1-57683-272-4

Cover design by Dan Jamison
Cover illustration by Susan Leopold / Lindgren & Smith
Creative Team: Nanci McAlister; Greg Clouse; Vicki Witte; Darla Hightower; Glynese Northam

Some of the anecdotal illustrations in this book are true to life and are included with the permission of the persons involved. All other illustrations are composites of real situations, and any resemblance to people living or dead is coincidental.

Unless otherwise identified, all Scripture quotations in this publication are taken from the *HOLY BIBLE: NEW INTERNATIONAL VERSION*® (NIV®). Copyright © 1973, 1978, 1984 by International Bible Society. Used by permission of Zondervan Publishing House. All rights reserved. Other versions used include: *The Message: New Testament with Psalms and Proverbs* (MSG) by Eugene H. Peterson, copyright © 1993, 1994, 1995, used by permission of NavPress Publishing Group; and the *Holy Bible, New Living Translation*, (NLT) copyright © 1996. Used by permission of Tyndale House Publishers, Inc., Wheaton, Illinois 60189. All rights reserved.

Moore, Kim, 1959-
    A patchwork heart : deepening your love for others / by Kim Moore and Pam Mellskog.
    p. cm.
Includes bibliographical references.
    ISBN 1-57683-272-4
    1. Caring. 2. Love. 3. Moore, Kim, 1959- I. Mellskog, Pam, 1967-
II. Title.
BJ1475 .M66 2002
241'.4–dc21   2002002123

Printed in the United States of America
1 2 3 4 5 6 7 8 9 10 / 05 04 03 02

FOR A FREE CATALOG OF
NAVPRESS BOOKS & BIBLE STUDIES,
CALL 1-800-366-7788 (USA)
OR 1-416-499-4615 (CANADA)

CONTENTS

FOREWORD

True compassion, generous grace, and tender mercy are some of the most encouraging, hope-giving, and faith-building gifts you can offer to another person. Compassion cares more for others than for self. It loves unconditionally, whatever the emotional, physical, or spiritual need might be. It doesn't have eyes to see race, religion, worthiness, or payback potential.

Compassion is the mirrored reflection of Christ in a human being trying to model what Jesus would do if He saw someone in need. It is the heart's response to lone-liness, pain, emptiness, hunger, ache, or oppression, combined with hands-on assistance that offers mercy, love, concern, and a path to healing and hope. Corrie ten Boom once said, "What did you do today that only a Christian would have done?"

Because of a devastating extended family crisis, I know what it feels like to experience this kind of love — a compassion you can never fully pay back, the kind that sits and weeps with you when the waiting is long and the journey is filled with deep sorrow. And I've also known Kim Moore long enough to assure you that her life demonstrates the principles she teaches.

With true stories and personal vulnerability, Kim and Pam will teach you how to develop your ability to follow in the footsteps of Christ, even if you don't have the gift of compassion. In addition to encouraging and affirming others, you'll discover how giving away pieces of your heart brings vitality, joy, fresh faith, and fulfillment to your own life.

Most of all, as you allow your heart to be entwined with Jesus', and with others as He taught and modeled, you'll appreciate the beauty that only a heaven-stitched patchwork can display.

Carol Kent, President
Speak Up Speaker Services and Author,
Becoming a Woman of Influence (NavPress)

Introduction: A Parable

One day a young woman stood in the town square and proclaimed that she had the most beautiful heart in the whole valley. A large crowd gathered, and they all admired her heart, for it was perfect, the most beautiful heart they had ever seen. There was not a mark or a flaw in it. The young woman was very proud and boasted all the more loudly. Suddenly, an old woman appeared at the front of the crowd.

"Why, your heart is not nearly as beautiful as mine," she said. The crowd and the young woman looked at the old woman's heart. It was beating strongly, but full of scars. It had places where pieces had been removed and other pieces put in. But they didn't fit quite right, and jagged edges abounded. In fact, in some places there were deep gouges where whole pieces were missing. The people stared and wondered how she could say her heart was more beautiful. When the young woman looked more closely at the old woman's heart, she laughed.

"You must be joking," she said. "Compare your heart with mine. Mine is perfect, and yours is a mess."

"Yes," agreed the old woman. "Yours is perfect-*looking*, but I would never trade. You see, every scar represents a person to whom I have given my love. I tear out a piece of my heart and give it to her, and often she gives me a piece of her heart that fits into the empty space. But because the pieces aren't exact I have some rough edges, which I cherish because they remind me of the love we shared.

"Sometimes I have given away pieces of my heart and the other person hasn't returned a piece of her heart to me. These are the empty gouges. Giving love is taking a chance. Although these gouges are painful, they stay open and remind me of the love I have for these people too. Perhaps someday they may yet fill the space I have waiting. So, now do you see what true beauty is?"

The young woman stood silently with tears running down her cheeks. She approached the old woman, reached into her own perfect and beautiful heart, and with trembling hands offered the old woman a generous piece.

The old woman accepted this offering and placed it in her heart, then took a piece from her scarred heart and placed it in the fresh wound of the young woman's heart. It fit, but not perfectly. There were some jagged edges.

The young woman looked at her heart, imperfect as it now was, and realized that it was more beautiful than ever. The two women embraced and walked away, side by side.

—Adapted, author unknown

This book is dedicated to helping you appreciate the value of a patchwork heart. By seeking God's compassion in your relationships with others, particularly with broken people, we predict you'll feel some pain. But the nicks and bruises symbolize the state of a working heart, a loving heart — a heart after God's heart. As you allow Him to expand the borders of your heart, so too shall you expand the borders of His kingdom. Blessings and peace to you in this ministry of tenderness and hope.

Sincerely,

KIM MOORE   PAM MELLSKOG
Plymouth, Michigan   Boulder, Colorado

Your Poor Choices
Are Not My Problem

When my husband, Eric, and I got the call from the hospital that night in 1983, the ER doctor gave no information except that his recently admitted patient had asked for us repeatedly. We arrived at Jae's bedside less than thirty minutes later expecting to find the nineteen-year-old coed suffering from yet another athletic injury.

Instead, we discovered Jae tied to a gurney without a scratch on her. In fact, she still wore street clothes.

When the deathly pale girl turned to face us, it confirmed that she was hospitalized more for mental reasons than physical ones. Streams of mascara ran down her cheeks and onto the pillow now smeared with rouge and makeup from her restless head tossing.

Between maniacal sobs and bursts of high laughter, she attempted to explain her situation. Yet, because she floated in and out of reality, she often struggled just to remember who we were and why we stood there watching her.

She seemed high, but on something stronger than marijuana, her drug of choice. Off the record, the doctor guessed that she had smoked some pot laced with LSD.

But by this point, she wasn't the only one on a bad trip. After I realized her life wasn't in danger, I started resenting that Jae's ongoing poor choices were becoming *my* problem. Ever since she arrived at the Christian university that fall, she had regularly violated curfew, abused drugs and alcohol, neglected her studies, and deprived her body of rest and a healthy diet.

Eric and I, then newlyweds, had graduated from the same university the year before. While he attended seminary nearby, we remained connected with the undergraduate students — Eric taught Speech 101, and I taught piano lessons. We spent more time with Jae than with most students, because she and I had grown up in the same town and attended the same church there.

We knew she was needy. At the hospital, we could see she was a mess. But her crying, vomiting, and hysterical babble only stoked my frustration. All sorts of self-righteous, judgmental thoughts crossed my mind as I stood at her bedside: *I told you this would happen if you didn't start making better choices. You made this hospital bed; why shouldn't you lie in it?*

Nonetheless, we stuck around until the wee hours of the morning for her release. During the interim, I sat in the waiting room and absentmindedly stared down a long empty hallway as I reflected on Jae's life to date.

She appeared to be a carefree, all-American girl. Short and muscular, she was a highschool softball star and serious enough about the sport to play it in college. No wonder. Besides talent, she brought an all-business attitude to her play.

On the field, she pulled her long blond hair back into a ponytail, tugged her cap down, and worked hard. Off the field, however, she dressed in the latest fashions and seemed to be perpetually on a diet trying to improve her looks. Jae wasn't beauty pageant gorgeous, but she was very cute — something her perky personality, southern drawl, and fun-loving sense of humor enhanced.

Winsome as she was in some ways, I still figured that

the university would expel her for this drug-related incident. If so, that would dash her hopes of both enjoying campus life and playing ball that spring — her two top priorities. I figured she deserved those consequences.

To pass the idle hours at the hospital, I extended my criticism and regrets about Jae to her family. They excelled at making poor choices too. For instance, all three of her older brothers had eventually gone to jail on drug possession charges. Her daddy was an alcoholic, and her mother had forged checks in the midst of divorcing him. Jae was thirteen at the time, and when the courts finalized the divorce, her parents fought over custody — neither wanted her to live with them.

So Jae struck a deal with her daddy. If he would pay her tuition at the Christian school she was attending at the time, she would move out. He agreed, and so every year of her high school career, she lived with a different family from our church.

Yawning and checking my watch, I mused more while Eric leafed through magazines. I could certainly concede that Jae grew up under some tough circumstances. But that did not mean I had to show her the same no-strings-attached compassion I would show, say, a tornado victim. It wasn't in my nature. Jae had graduated from high school and cut ties with her family. She wasn't a victim. She alone was responsible for her actions.

That's how I typically responded to "messy" people like Jae. I even joked with friends that when God handed out compassion, He must have skipped me because I always came up empty-handed. As an adult, my heart hardened more toward needy people. However, at the literal midnight hour, God used an old memory to begin cracking my long-entrenched critical spirit. The memory that floated in was of Jae as a funny, cuddly five-year-old girl riding my daddy's bus to church.

Her great uncle served as a deacon with my father at our church. Though her parents passed on invitations to the service, they happily shipped Jae and her brothers off to Sunday school every week. To them, it probably seemed like the ultimate godsend — free baby-sitting for their four kids every Sunday morning! My daddy would pull the church bus up to the curb in front of their house and honk the horn, and down the sidewalk the kids would bound excitedly. When the boys hit junior high, they stopped coming. But Jae kept riding the bus, or she arranged to get rides from friends, until she left for college.

When I remembered Jae's expectant face as she jumped onto the bus with her brothers — the hope in her — I slowly began thinking about compassion in a different way. It dawned on me that God still saw Jae as that adorable five-year-old, as His child. He also saw her poor choices and loved her no less. There's no way He would want her freaked out on drugs, but that wouldn't blind Him from caring about her.

It took another ten years for me to fully appreciate and adopt this perspective — to see needy people with compassion though Jesus' eyes. But more about that in the next chapter.

Still, I surprised myself that night when the graveyard shift doctor appeared at long last to release his strung-out charge. I took Jae home for the night and even invited her to live with us — something she did for the next two years.

The only explanation I could offer for such uncharacteristic compassion-in-action stemmed from our childhood connection. I could see into Jae's past to understand her present. But God was calling me to see all people like Jae with the eyes of faith — to show compassion regardless of how much history I knew.

The Roots of Compassion

In recent years, a fascinating new branch of Christian education has revolved around discovering giftedness — in leadership, communication, giving, discernment, and so on. At least that explains why some people never struggle to show compassion to strangers — God has given them the gift of mercy.

The gift of mercy has been described as "the divine enablement to cheerfully and practically help those who are suffering or are in need. [It is] compassion in action."[1] People with this gift focus on alleviating the sources of pain or discomfort in suffering people. They address the needs of the lonely and forgotten; express love, grace, and dignity to those facing hardships and crisis; and serve in difficult or unsightly circumstances, doing so cheerfully. They also concern themselves with individual and social issues that oppress people.

But not having that gift of mercy doesn't excuse the rest of us from showing compassion. Loving others is essential to every person no matter what gift of the Spirit she is blessed with. For instance, I have a gift of discernment that is very helpful as I pray with people or advise them spiritually. Yet if I approach the use of this gift without allowing God to love people through me, I can hurt them even further. There have been plenty of times when I've wanted to say, "Look, do I have to write this on the wall for you, buddy?" It's so obvious to me what needs to be corrected, and somehow they just don't see it.

Slowly I've learned that not everything I discern needs to be communicated immediately. Yes, people need to know the truth, but *how* I present that truth will either aid or destroy the opportunity for help and healing. That's where compassion comes in. With God's help I can be more patient, less judgmental, and abundantly forbearing — great tools in the hands of the Master. The use of my Spirit-empowered gifts will undoubtedly help the kingdom's cause only as they are accompanied by compassion toward others.

Clearly, I don't have the mercy gift. However, during the past five years, as I've made myself more available to God, He has taken that availability and helped me to see what can happen in the lives of the people in my world if I will just be willing to give away a piece of my heart. The key has been *allowing* God to reshape my heart, thus enhancing my ability to love.

Stepping-Stones to God's Heart

What exactly does a patchwork heart look like? When Jesus told the Parable of the Good Samaritan, He said that the essence of the Ten Commandments is to "love the Lord your God with all your heart and with all your soul and with all your strength and with all your mind" and to "love your neighbor as yourself" (Luke 10:27). This simple sentence captures God's top priorities — then and now. He wants us to love Him and to love the people He has created. That's easier said than done. However, with faith and God's grace — and a commitment to obeying His Word — showing compassion *can* happen.

Jesus told His disciples, "Whoever has my commands and obeys them, he is the one who loves me. He who loves me will be loved by my Father, and I too will love him and show myself to him" (John 14:21). John restated this truth in his first epistle: "If someone claims, 'I know him (God) well!' but doesn't keep his commandments, he's obviously a liar. His life doesn't match his words. But the one who keeps God's word is the person in whom we see God's mature love. This is the only way to be sure we're in God. Anyone who claims to be intimate with God ought to live the same kind of life Jesus lived" (1 John 2:3-6, MSG).

Yet, how easy it is to look past these Scriptures and resent neediness and brokenness in a hurting person! At the very least, Eric and I lost a good night's sleep as we waited for the hospital to release Jae. But our actions that night illustrate a mystery of Christian faith: the things that seem like stumbling blocks may really be stepping-stones. To what? To God's heart. As John wrote, "If anyone says, 'I love God,' yet hates his brother, he is a liar. For anyone who does not love his brother, whom he has seen, cannot love God, whom he has not seen" (1 John 4:20).

At first glance, the rewards of compassion rarely seem to tip the scales in favor of the giver. For instance, Jesus wept with compassion over Jerusalem — the city that would stage His brutal murder. Yet He saw past the sacrifice to the victory of doing God's will.

Regardless of a person's poor choices or unfortunate circumstances, being willing to practice compassion makes a bridge to God's heart and creates the type of relationship that He desires. That's why learning to respond with compassion-in-action begins with a desire to see needy folks from Christ's perspective — instead of with self-righteous criticism.

Noted author Ken Gire sums it up well:

Before we can love our neighbor, we must *see* our neighbor and *hear* our neighbor. Observing the way a gardener observes plants. Watching their buds when they're blooming. Watering their roots when they're wilting. But we cannot weep with those who weep or rejoice with those who rejoice unless we first see something of their tears or hear something of their laughter. If we can learn to see and hear our neighbor, maybe, just maybe, we can learn to see and hear God. And seeing him and hearing him, to love Him.[2]

Chapter One

When I asked God to expand the borders of my heart so that I could better see needy people the way Jesus sees them, I never expected how He would take me up on that prayer! Honestly, if I had known what was ahead, I'm quite sure I wouldn't have had the courage to utter the words I sent to heaven that day in 1990. But God, who is most definitely rich in mercy, chose to answer my prayer for compassion. And that answer has completely and radically changed my life — and the lives of others.

2

Switching Places

In 1994, Eric and I ducked into a movie theater to see *Shadowlands*, Hollywood's portrayal of the life of British theologian C. S. Lewis. We had read many of his books over the years and greatly admired his imaginative fiction and eloquent Christian apologetics. But this film was based on a play by the same name that revolved around Lewis's love life, of all things. I tucked some Kleenex into my purse in case it turned out to be a tearjerker, and we settled into our seats with a cardboard tray of popcorn and Cokes.

In the first scene Lewis addresses an auditorium full of religious educators all masked with deadpan expressions. As he lectures on the problem of pain, his controlled voice echoes off the walls. He concludes that when pain happens, one must simply turn to God. Then, he steps away from the podium.

About mid-scene, I leaned further back on the velvet upholstery and stopped munching. Lewis's dry comments showed precious little compassion for those of us confused and disheartened by suffering. Life hadn't been easy for me lately, and all his answers to the problem of pain seemed disappointingly pat.

It becomes clear as the movie rolls that had this esteemed professor stayed in his ivory tower at Oxford

University, he could have remained aloof indefinitely. Instead, he meets Joy Davidman and falls in love for the first time in the autumn of his life. His passion for this beautiful, brassy American expatriate surprises him, but perhaps not as much as his pain when they soon learn that she's ill with a fast-acting terminal cancer.

The movie takes a major tack when Lewis begins grappling with up-close-and-personal pain versus poking at it with the quill of academia. And he ultimately learns what I have since begun learning: the depth of your pain correlates very closely to the depth of your love for others.

I was a late bloomer in this process. After all, up until the early nineties — when I turned thirty — I acted like Lewis did before he met Joy. I figured life's toughest trials either didn't apply to me or simply required a more enlightened spiritual approach. I took life by the horns and solved my problems with confidence and a certain detachment. Why couldn't everyone else do the same? If I lived my life by the Book, I trusted that everything would work out to my advantage, that blessing would surely follow obedience.

The future held a rude awakening for me. In April 1989, I happily brought that paint-by-numbers mentality to our new ministry in Canton, Michigan. Eric and I moved there to start a church for unchurched people and, initially, this work seemed romantic and exciting. I pictured what the building would look like and even how people would interact there. The Acts 2 church could blossom again, this time in Canton, and I hoped thousands of people would flock to hear Eric's messages and respond to God's leading in their lives. Furthermore, unlike some other new converts, ours wouldn't dillydally in plugging into small group Bible studies to be discipled to spiritual maturity.

After all, God had called our church to be a beacon of light in the fog of a spiritually dark community. Surely He would help us build a huge ministry facility and hire the most innovative, progressive staff to do cutting-edge ministry. Unfortunately, God had other plans, many of which involved transforming my ministry fantasies into a more nitty-gritty understanding of needy people.

From the beginning, this church plant stretched us tightly. In fact, we had no money and only three other couples in attendance when we opened the doors. But we were young and full of faith, so we rolled up our sleeves in hopes that others would eventually catch our ministry vision.

Sure enough, attendance jumped from six regulars to sixty-five to a hundred in less than a year. We considered these growth spurts absolutely miraculous. But there was a downside to planting a church that met our stated mission. While we effectively attracted the unchurched, that brought a more secular dynamic to the fellowship mix. I confess that I shook many hands without sensing the compassion of Christ in my heart.

For instance, I remember standing in the lobby of the school we rented on weekends and chatting with a couple that regularly showed up. I asked them at some point about how long they had been married. "Oh, we're not married," they replied and then smiled pleasantly at each other. "We've been together for about eight years now, but we're still not sure about the whole marriage thing." Living together constituted no moral dilemma for them. Rather, it seemed prudent. They enjoyed being with each other, but both feared marriage. Why not just cohabit? I hoped the shock this bona fide church lady felt didn't register as I struggled to maintain my end of the small talk.

Why are you coming to church if you're blatantly disobeying God? I wondered as the subject switched to home mortgage interest rates. Before we parted, I had already tattooed a scarlet letter on their foreheads. They were marked people. They were the bad sinners.

Another time, I spoke with a woman bemoaning her

troubled life. About twenty minutes into the saga, I started tuning out and formulating my exit comment: "Hello? I've got a bit of wisdom for you here, lady. Don't make the same stupid decisions, and you won't get the same stupid results."

I found my judgmental and impatient attitude creep like a Jeep on steep rocks. Before I knew it, I was sick and tired of dealing with these messy unchurched folks — especially since they all started sounding like the same broken record of one dysfunctional life issue or another. Frankly, with only a thimbleful of compassion, I failed to appreciate that God had handpicked the congregation and dropped them on our church's doorstep for a reason.

But I didn't sign up for this assignment! I inwardly protested. I wanted to meet the unchurched people who had their personal problems under control. Instead, the bulk of our church crowd needed counsel, prayer, and Bible 101 lessons. They didn't know the difference between the Old Testament and the New Testament. I can now relate to how Jacob felt at his wedding when he lifted the veil and found homely Leah, not ravishing Rachel. I felt as if God had delivered the wrong bride to Eric and me — and I definitely felt jilted!

Then one afternoon, God invaded my thoughts. He reminded me of the time when He placed His call on my life. I had told Him I would serve Him anytime, anyplace, to anyone. Yep. I had said those words and meant them. Deep down in my heart I still meant them, but something wasn't working properly. If folks didn't fit in my tiny box, if they didn't mirror my value system and my priorities, I brushed them off. I had little concern and less compassion for them. Why waste time getting closer?

As you can imagine, such an attitude posed a monumental stumbling block for someone committed to vocational ministry. But by God's grace, I pled for soul surgery. I turned toward heaven and prayed that God would change my life by expanding the borders of my heart. I wanted to love people the way He loved them. I wanted to be able to give them something of Him, but it was very apparent to me that there was a part of Him that I did not yet possess. I offered that prayer and then promptly forgot about it, but God didn't. He began orchestrating events in my life that would fulfill His desires for that prayer — like it or not.

The Hurt That Began the Healing

Four years after our move to Canton, as I sat next to Eric in that dark theater watching *Shadowlands,* I realized with a deep sense of dejection that something had gotten lost along the way for me. I wasn't sure exactly how it had happened, but I found that cynicism had captured and shrink-wrapped my heart. And I felt dustier than C. S. Lewis sounded in the opening scene.

When had I begun to stray so far from Jesus' example and teaching in the area of compassion? I hit my mental rewind button and realized that the hardening of my heart must have started as we finished our first year in Michigan. That's when I first found myself switching places, sliding uncontrollably from the role of a put-together, can-do person into the role of a broken, weepy person.

I was almost halfway through my third pregnancy, and we were all very excited about our new family addition. Lincoln, our tenderhearted firstborn, was four years old and hoping against hope that this baby would be a boy. Meanwhile, two-year-old Brittany, a 100 percent nurturer, gleefully anticipated rocking a real baby.

Although our grassroots ministry tried all our resources, home remained a haven and our kids were a constant source of hilarity and blessing. So I dreamed of having a house overflowing with children and counted the days to the birthday of baby number three.

The sun shone brightly on the day of my ultrasound appointment, and it cheered me when Eric and the kids at the last minute piled in the car. As we motored to the medical building a few miles from our house, Lincoln and Brittany couldn't wait to glimpse their new brother or sister.

It was a routine ultrasound for the midway point of pregnancy, so I felt familiar with the procedure. I relaxed and stretched out on the table as I watched the technician move the wand over my ever-growing abdomen. Then her bubbly chitchat abruptly stopped, and she squinted at the computer monitor.

"Is there a problem?" I asked, jerking my head up.

"I can't really say at this point. Give me a minute here," she distractedly replied. After taking a couple of pictures, she carefully laid the wand down and faced me. Could I immediately go upstairs to review the scan results with a doctor?

I nodded, and several minutes later Eric and I sat in the doctor's office waiting for her to confirm what we dreaded. The doctor practically tiptoed in and then gingerly sat on her desk. She stared intently at us as she struggled to find the right words.

"I'm afraid . . . I am afraid we've lost the baby, Mr. and Mrs. Moore," she said at last. "I am so sorry."

It felt like someone had poured ice-cold water into my veins. I went numb all over. Eric worked out the arrangements for me to check into the hospital later that day. As I recuperated from delivering stillborn little Kelsey, my doctor reappeared in my room and spoke reassuring words in hushed tones. She explained that despite losing this baby, I was still young and healthy. She didn't see any reason why I couldn't carry another baby to term. Before leaving to finish her rounds, she encouraged me to give my body a couple of months to heal. Then, whenever I felt ready, I could try to get pregnant.

By the beginning of the summer, we rejoiced to discover that I was with child once again. All the usual pregnancy symptoms appeared, so I trusted that we'd end up with a healthy baby this time. We heard a strong heartbeat at the August checkup, which zapped any anxious thoughts. Surely this baby adventure would turn out OK. I felt so confident that we took a vacation to visit friends on the East Coast.

Soon after returning to Michigan, I had another checkup. Everything looked great. The baby's heartbeat drummed along, and I was popping out more every day. Before leaving the clinic, we set up an appointment for the next ultrasound on October 23, just five days before my birthday. That date would be twenty weeks from concep-tion, a little later than normal due to scheduling conflicts. The upside was that we could know the baby's gender by then. As I made the appointment, I remember smiling. That news would be an extra-special early birthday present for me that year.

When October 23 rolled around, we all hopped in the car and trekked to the hospital again. Staff ushered me into the ultrasound room, and in less than five minutes, we were looking at the baby. When the gregarious doctor stopped talking mid-sentence, I knew something was not right.

"Is there something unusual there?" I asked. He fum-bled with the wand and muttered something about the equipment giving him fits. I didn't buy it, though.

"What is the matter?" I probed, seconds later.

He put down the wand and paused a moment before looking at me. The minute my eyes hit his, I knew what he was going to say. I had seen that look before.

"Something's wrong," I whispered, tears already streaming down my cheeks.

"Yes, something is wrong. Kim, the baby's heartbeat is gone. The baby's there and looks fine, but we don't have a heartbeat."

He called in another doctor for a second opinion, and together they confirmed that the baby had died. They brought Eric in from the lobby and plans were made for me to deliver that day. It all seemed surreal. Activity swirled around me, but time stood still in my world. It was like sinking to the bottom of the ocean and sitting trancelike in darkness, almost completely insulated from the surface activity. My spirit looked heavenward to express just one word: "Why?"

Labor complications intensified the emotional loss, but by 10:30 that evening, I had delivered a tiny boy we named William Morgan after my great-grandfather, a circuit-riding preacher. He looked perfect for a twenty-week-old baby — except for the obvious.

Just before I checked out the next morning, my doctor appeared. He carefully sat on the edge of my bed and explained his concerns about future pregnancies. Fetal death syndrome, not a miscarriage, caused my two tragedies. Therefore, he asked me to reevaluate my dream of bearing more children. As he stood to leave, he advised me to at least wait before trying to get pregnant, to rest. I should also prepare myself emotionally for the possibility of never carrying another baby to term.

Like the proverbial straw that broke the camel's back, something inside me just snapped at the news. I yearned to race to the highest mountain and scream, "This isn't fair!" I opted instead to cry my eyes out. When a friend lost her baby, I had commented to my girlfriends that without the baby in the crook of my arm I probably wouldn't have the strength to walk out of the hospital. Now I had done it not once, but twice, in a year's time.

Friends and family provided so much love and support during those first few days after I came home. I was very weak and sleepy, so they took over the household duties and watched my kids. The physical healing happened quickly. But when the haze finally lifted and life settled back into a routine, my terrifying internal struggle began. A strange anger had taken root when I read William's autopsy, and in the disorientation that grief brings, I let that anger grow. The only one I could blame was God. After all, He gives and takes life. It was His choice to take Kelsey and William, and I just couldn't fathom why.

The thing that really ticked me off was that I had sacrificed so much to follow God's leading in my life. I had left my close-knit family in sunny Texas and moved to dreary Michigan. I had indefinitely shelved my musical aspirations to help my husband start a seeker-sensitive church. I had faithfully lived the Christian life since childhood. I regularly attended church, read the Bible, participated in Bible studies, ministered in a variety of settings, prayed, and even fasted now and then.

In a twisted way, I felt God owed me. I had been waiting in the blessing line way too long, and all I seemed to be getting was grief. I told God how disappointed I was in Him, how He had let me down. I added that I didn't know if I wanted to serve Him anymore. If this was all the reward I got, I was prepared to officially hand Him my resignation.

Those were absolutely the darkest days as I grieved the loss of two children, struggled to help Eric run the new church, and worried about our mounting debts — including the hefty doctor bills. My anger at God only complicated my feelings of isolation and loneliness. Finding comfort in the midst of all of that distress seemed impossible.

So I languished. I fell into a serious depression that led me down a path toward suicide. Instead of caring well for the two darling children God had already blessed me with, I fought just to get out of bed every morning. A persistent numbness marked most of my waking hours, and even making simple conversation taxed my abilities.

I tried to keep my dangerous condition between God

and me, but volcanic eruptions of anger became more frequent and uncontrollable. In this way, I hurt everyone — including the ones I loved most. Eric soon became concerned and asked me to get some help. As I began to peel back the layers of my grief and anger with our counselor, I made steady progress. And I learned how to process those emotions with Eric instead of without him.

The Great Exchange

But I still felt trapped until I heard Patsy Clairmont — a regular speaker on the "Women of Faith" tour — address the audience at Spring Hill Camp's Women's Retreat. After she shared her own story, I asked to bend her ear. I yearned to be free from my anger, and she seemed to have the kind of insight I needed. When she kindly agreed to listen, I told her the whole story of how I had gone from smug self-sufficiency to desperate brokenness in less than a year.

A box of tissues later, Patsy wisely suggested that perhaps I had begun believing some things about God that weren't true.

"I don't think so," I replied, trying to wipe the "Who me?" expression off my face.

Not being put off by my bravado, she continued: "Well, it seems to me that you think God is picking on you, that He is purposefully holding back information that would help you out of this mess; am I right?" She and I both knew the answer to that question without me even opening my mouth. "So what do you do with the verse in James 1 that says, 'If any of you lacks wisdom, he should ask God, who gives generously to all without finding fault, and it will be given to him'?" (verse 5).

Feeling like the child caught with her hand in the cookie jar, I sheepishly looked up, realizing that once again I had fallen for one of the Enemy's schemes.

Immediately my mind was flooded with the inner thoughts that had been a part of my world for too long: *God had deserted me in my darkest hour. God's heart wasn't good toward me. God was punishing me and wouldn't tell me why. I would never be happy again because of these circumstances. I would always be depressed.*

"Do you believe that God's Word is true?"

Patsy's question brought me back to reality. "Well, yes, of course I do."

She smiled. "Then I have a homework assignment for you."

Scrambling home from that retreat I sat myself down at the kitchen table with a new notebook and began to write. Following Patsy's advice I made two columns. On the left side of the page in big letters I wrote *lies*, and across from that column in bigger letters, I wrote *truth*. Listing the lies that had been running in my head under the appropriate column, I then turned to God's Word and sought out the truth. I was astounded at what I found.

God had not deserted me; in fact He was very close. "The righteous cry out, and the LORD hears them; he delivers them from all their troubles. The LORD is close to the brokenhearted and saves those who are crushed in spirit" (Psalm 34:17-18).

God's heart was indeed good toward me. "For the LORD God is a sun and shield; the LORD bestows favor and honor; no good thing does he withhold from those whose walk is blameless" (Psalm 84:11).

I realized that God's heart was bent toward me after reading in the book of Joel how lovingly God restored Israel when they repented from their sin. His generous spirit was evident when He promised to replace all that they had lost because of their own disobedience: "I will repay you for the years the locusts have eaten. . . . You will have plenty to eat, until you are full . . . never again will my people be shamed"

(Joel 2:25-26). Those became sweet words to my spirit.

As I began to receive God's truth as my truth, my disappointment and anger began to slip away. I had always believed that God's Word was alive, but that phrase took on new meaning as its power began to work miracles in my inner world. It seemed every time I picked up the Scripture, God's Spirit spoke to me through a text I found. My mind was being renewed and my heart was changing in the process. As God expressed His compassion for me and I received it from Him, there was a great exchange. Not only did I possess what I had been given, but there was also an increased capacity and even a *desire* to share what I had with others.

A New Piece of My Heart

I first realized this newfound compassion where none had been before in 1995 following one of our Sunday morning services. A woman I had never met before approached me and soon poured out her heart. At the time, our church met in a high school. I was in charge of the auditorium teardown, so it wasn't a very convenient time for me to take five. But I found myself delegating the teardown job to someone else and handing off my toddler son Hunter (God is still in the miracle-making business!) to step aside and give her my full attention.

I listened intently to her problems and offered what I hoped would be helpful counsel. Before parting company, I also asked if I could pray for her. As I prayed, I began to sense God's heart for this dear hurting person that He loved so much. Instead of resenting her sense of helplessness and fear, I found myself being driven to tears for her. It was as if all the events of the past two hardscrabble years came into focus. Why? I prayed for the first time in my life with an intimate understanding of pain — and compassion followed. Walking away from that encounter, I realized with bittersweet appreciation that God had answered an old prayer of mine. He had finally expanded the borders of my heart so I could love people more deeply. There was something of Him that had been planted in me as I endured my great pain, and that piece of Him now became a treasure to be given to my hurting friend.

"Getting into the stride of God means nothing less than union with Himself," wrote Oswald Chambers. "It takes a long time to get there, but keep at it. Don't give in because the pain is bad just now, get on with it, and before long you will find you have a new vision and a new purpose."[1]

Yet, hurting people often go anywhere but to God for pain relief. For instance, a gazillion restaurants serve your favorite comfort foods, plenty of time-consuming projects exist to gobble up your free time, and big-ticket toys — like a new car, boat, or house — make instant gratification seem possible. My favorite way to dull the pain was shopping at the mall — a new outfit seemed to do the trick nicely, at least for a few hours.

But by delving into these coping mechanisms, you may miss *the* thing God is trying to do through your pain. Furthermore, quick fixes offer short-term relief, but they can also short-circuit the healing process and extend the hurt. The apostle James offered comforting clarification:

> Consider it a sheer gift, friends, when tests and challenges come at you from all sides. You know that under pressure, your faith-life is forced into the open and shows its true colors. So don't try to get out of anything prematurely. Let it do its work so you become mature and well-developed, not deficient in any way. (1:2-4, MSG)

God's encouragement runs counter-intuitive to everything our bodies tell us to do. He whispers that there simply aren't enough trinkets to do the work that only He can accomplish. He wants us to lean into Him, not buy something, eat something, read something, or sleep! He wants us to lay our weary heads on the table and cry our eyes out if we must, but then fall into His arms as many times as needed so that we can feel the holy hug from heaven that brings healing to our souls. It is in those moments that the transfer of God's heart will happen, breaking into our pain and radically transforming our inner world.

We must be courageous enough to let pain do its work, and brave enough to endure so that our hearts become filled to overflowing with God's infinite and complete love. Then, and only then, will we be able to look into the eyes of a hurting brother or sister and know what it feels like to switch places.

3

COMPASSION'S
HALL OF FAME

I wanted to pinch myself. Could I be flying to one of my favorite places? The captain's voice soon confirmed an on-time arrival in Nashville that afternoon, so I let my head lazily loll to the side as I watched *terra firma* shrink away from the plane's cubby window.

Every year, the Gospel Music Association hosts a con-vention in this Mecca of Christian music. Since 1995, the Academy of Gospel Music Arts has designed a seminar for music ministry newbies within this convention. I didn't know exactly what to expect, but I wanted my husband, Eric, to floor the rental car once we arrived. Heavy traffic quickly snarled a speedy commute from the airport. Yet, my friendly chauffeur-husband managed to drop me off very close to the ritzy Stouffer Hotel so I could register on time.

I only needed to go around the corner and walk about a half block. That's when I spotted what appeared to be a misplaced cattle guard. This sidewalk grate stretched from the curb to the building foundations. The fan below wasn't blowing at the time. However, that day I wore a broom-skirted dress and knew to scoot or else tempt an unplanned Marilyn Monroe-like cameo.

Oh, cruel fate. Just as I reached the halfway mark with

quick ladylike footsteps, a monstrous fan roared to life. The warm blast billowed the dress despite my frantic scramble to the other side of what now seemed like the Grand Canyon. Nevertheless, I hastily marched on when I reached the concrete because I was too embarrassed to thoroughly inspect.

Engrossed in my disheveled appearance, I rounded the corner and scarcely glanced at the two well-heeled men approaching. But out of the corner of my eye, their expressions told me that I indeed needed to fix a few things. I peered at my reflection in the nearest window as they wordlessly passed. The skirt had fallen back in place, but the underskirt had bunched into a bulge around my hips the size of Goodyear's largest tire. Never mind that this made the skirt see-through.

Mortified, I cozied up to the potted tree on the corner and slyly scanned both directions for pedestrians. The coast was clear. So I frantically made the necessary adjustments. Satisfied at last, I snuck away from the wall and then sauntered toward the hotel's elegant floor-to-ceiling glass and brass main entrance.

It was then that I realized that the Stouffer Hotel has a restaurant below street level, with a long row of windows to make it easier for me to flash those lovely people trying to eat dinner. This was not the lasting impression I had hoped to make.

The humiliation didn't stop there. When I finally graced the hotel lobby with my presence and scoped out the room, I felt like a Baptist at a swing dance. This scene looked more like New York City than Nashville, with everyone hustling and bustling to their next appointment or chatting on their cell phones.

Compulsively patting my renegade broom-skirt dress in place once more, I instinctively understood that they were the "haves," and that I was the "have-not" at this bash.

Though I managed to mingle amid the forest of chic forms, I felt stuck on the outside looking in.

While my momentary embarrassment was uncomfortable, it would only register about a 1.5 on the Richter scale of pain. It was fleeting, not permanent, and completely, if not humiliatingly, endurable. I suspect some people live with that sinking outside-looking-in perspective every day. Instead of occasionally feeling like a duck out of water, they never find a pond in which to splash around and get comfortable — let alone happy.

When I am painfully honest, it is not hard to find people in my world — people to whom life has not been gentle — struggling more profoundly than I did at the Stouffer Hotel. Some ooze with neediness. I admit that when the phone rings, I often sigh before taking their call because I know our conversation will be anything but lighthearted and uplifting.

I call them the "messy" people, and they tap the last drops of my inherently low patience supply. For when all is said and done, there are no simple solutions, no quick-fix remedies to their tangled situations. They desperately need ongoing support and friendship. Yet most lack good relational skills, making it all the tougher to hang in there with them.

Frustrated with what I know in my head to be less than spiritually mature behavior, I ask God regularly for a change of heart. How can I be compassionate, genuinely compassionate, when He introduces me to difficult people? Where can I find the abiding patience necessary for dealing with messy characters? How do I humble myself enough to love and not judge? Is it really possible to be the hands and feet of Jesus?

Peter's second epistle teaches, "His divine power has given us *everything* we need for life and godliness through our knowledge of him who called us by his own glory and goodness" (2 Peter 1:3, emphasis mine). If that is so, I must trust that compassion, just like love, humility, and other spiritual traits, can and should become a bigger part of my daily life. When you are ready to listen and learn, when you give God an attentive heart, He is always available to show you the "how to's" of developing this beautiful Christlike quality. Switching places — needing compassion versus just showing it — will certainly sensitize you. But beyond that, compassion comes when you bring fresh eyes to life's most ordinary scenery.

My son Hunter taught me that one sunny morning when he was just three years old. During our weekly jaunt to Target to troll for treasures, I heard his sweet voice mumbling from the backseat. I glanced at the rearview mirror and noticed that, though strapped in like a hostage, he had nevertheless craned his neck to see out the window.

With one tiny finger, he pointed toward the white cotton candy clouds littering the azure blue sky and whispered," There's a dinosaur. And there's a monkey. And there's a Popsicle. And there's a tree." I wondered if the child was hallucinating. But upon closer inspection, I realized that all of those things were plainly visible in the clouds drifting so high above. It was just a matter of slowing down long enough (while keeping one eye on the road, of course!) to really see them. The same goes for seeing the world as God sees it.

God says, "My thoughts are not your thoughts, neither are your ways my ways" (Isaiah 55:8). Because of that simple truth, you need to ask Him to reveal what He wants you to see. How can you begin that process? That's a good question with a simple answer — look at His Son first.

Learning from the Savior

As early as age twelve, when Mary and Joseph found their "lost" son teaching in the synagogue, Jesus knew He needed to be about His Father's business. Judging from the gospel accounts, much of that business had to do with compassion:

> When he saw the crowds, he had compassion on them, because they were harassed and helpless, like sheep without a shepherd (Matthew 9:36).

> When Jesus landed and saw a large crowd, he had compassion on them and healed their sick (Matthew 14:14).

> Filled with compassion, Jesus reached out his hand and touched the man (Mark 1:41).

> "I (Jesus) have compassion for these people; they have already been with me three days and have nothing to eat" (Mark 8:2).

One afternoon, I decided to dig a little deeper into these texts. So, I hopped in my car and showed up on my pastor's doorstep. Lucky for me, he's my husband too! I'm not a Greek scholar, so I asked him to help me find the meaning of "compassion." Eric took a break, and we pored over several dictionaries.

There are two words used in the Greek for compassion. One of them, *oiktirmos*,[1] is found in Romans 9:15: "For he (God) says to Moses, 'I will have mercy on whom I have mercy, and I will have compassion on whom I have compassion.'" Here the word compassion speaks of the kind of love and concern God possesses. It describes an aspect of His character. He simply *is* compassion, as He is just, faithful, and merciful. In every way He embodies compassion in its purest form and with complete integrity.

The other Greek word used is *splanchnon* (try to say

that three times fast). This word means to be moved inwardly, emotionally, and is used of Christ when He was moved with compassion toward people. Several times in the New Testament we see Jesus moved to tears: when He saw the people mourning the death of Lazarus (John 11), when He looked out over Jerusalem (Matthew 23), and before He performed the miracle of feeding the five thousand with a little boy's lunch (Matthew 14). Each time the word used is *splanchnon.*

Things get really interesting in Colossians 3:12, where Paul writes, "Therefore, as God's chosen people, holy and dearly loved, clothe yourselves with compassion, kindness, humility, gentleness and patience." Here again the word is *oiktirmos.* As Eric and I read this leaning over his desk, we both had one of those "Aha!" moments. Scripture says that we are to clothe ourselves with God's compassion. God is willing to develop His compassion in us if we are willing to receive it. That's exactly what happened with Jesus. He was the embodiment of God's character on earth. He clothed Himself with *oiktirmos* (His Father's compassion that was given to Him because He was willing to be about His Father's business), and because He was filled with God's compassion, He then was able to show *splanchnon* to those around Him.

This is great news for the compassionately challenged. Essentially, what we learn here is that we don't possess enough love and concern within ourselves to continually give to the people in our lives. But God has an unending amount of compassion that He is more than willing to share. Remember, He has given us everything we need for life and godliness! It's as if God has a well of compassion within Him and He says to us, "Come and drink, let me fill you up." When we are humble enough to allow God to fill us with His love, a miracle happens. We find an extra reserve of patience for that difficult individual. We can look into the eyes of a homeless person, see the person God wants him to be, and not pass judgment. This is a gift that only God can give.

Learning from Others

If you're like me, it is always helpful when learning something new to learn from others. Many of life's practical lessons are learned from watching others, whether it's our parents, teachers, pastors, friends, or job supervisors. If we are to become people of compassion, it is wise for us to look around and notice the people who already embody this trait. For me these otherwise ordinary mortals qualify for my "Compassion's Hall of Fame." I give them that honor not only for the way they integrate these two Greek definitions, but also because they clearly understand that the first step of compassion involves getting uncomfortably close to unmet needs.

Not surprisingly, the late Mother Teresa earns the top spot on my list. Arriving in Calcutta, India, from her native Macedonia in her twenties, she spent the rest of her days ministering with compassion to the outcasts of society. She and the order of nuns she founded built orphanages, hospitals, and hospices in India and around the world.

Once, when walking through the streets with these devoted sisters, Mother Teresa came upon a desperately ill, poverty-stricken woman. Rats nibbled at her flesh and — weak from hunger and disease — she could not shoo them away. The sisters picked her up and took her to the House of Compassion to nurse her back to good health. Later, the press asked Mother Teresa how she and her cadre could tolerate touching such a person.

"I could not have been a Missionary of Charity if I had passed by when I saw and smelt that woman who was eaten up by rats — her face, her legs," the stooped lady in flowing blue-and-white garb replied. "But I returned, picked her up and took her to the hospital. If I had not, the Society would have died. Feelings of repugnance are human, but if I see the face of Jesus in His most distressing disguise, I will be holy."[2]

Such faith both inspires and overwhelms me. No doubt, God gifted Mother Teresa with a tremendous capacity to love. In obedience to Him, she followed her calling with great courage and perseverance until He took her home in 1997. But being a perfectionist, I can slide into the all-or-nothing trap. If I can't show compassion like this nun, then why bother?

Yet, God's been teaching me that compassion can be expressed in very individual ways. It will look one way in me, another way in my sister, my husband, or in you. The fact is, God doesn't want me to go to India — at least not now. He wants to show His compassion through me right here in my suburban Detroit community. And He wants to do the same through you right where you are as well.

Sometimes our life experiences help us find ways to be compassionate. My mother, Shirley Buffington, another member of my hall of fame, is a perfect example of taking difficult life circumstances and finding a way to show compassion through them. After suffering so much neglect and abuse as a child, she could have run from it as an adult. Instead, she chose to shower others with the love and compassion that comes from close encounters with pain.

Mom grew up on a Kansas scratch farm during the Great Depression. The country's hard economic times were bad enough, but her father made life ten times worse. This man abused his family in almost every way possible. He bubbled with rage and viewed children as valuable only to the degree that they could labor in the fields.

It complicated life for my mom when her father blamed her for a household accident that resulted in the death of her sister. Though my mother was an infant at the time — not old enough to do anyone serious harm — my grandfather refused to acknowledge his own poor judgment and take responsibility for the tragedy. Instead, he blamed my mother forever.

His hostile rejection scarred her, but she decided in her early twenties to choose a better way of life — a life of compassion, not cruelty. Not surprisingly, she chose to focus on serving children. She's spent nearly four decades teaching children in Sunday school about Jesus, the kindest Friend a kid could have. Thirty-eight years is a long time to sit at a miniature table on a munchkin chair teaching Bible stories and giving away pieces of your heart. But she missed loving adult interaction as a child, and this ministry gives her a chance to make a positive difference by prizing another generation of children. It is compassion that has led her down this long road of obedience.

Though I'm not yet eligible for Compassion's Hall of Fame, I too have personally experienced the power life situations can play in shaping a patchwork heart. One such defining moment occurred October 15, 2000. After my morning prayers that day, I gazed out the window at our backyard and let the quiet sliver of peacefulness gently pry open my mind. That's when I sensed God calling me to arrange a concert for prisoners.

I looked at the floor and hoped I was mistaken. Like most, I try to sidestep pain and problems. But God seemed to smile and nod at this outreach idea. After all, an acquaintance of mine currently sat in a maximum-security facility in Orlando, Florida, awaiting trial.

As a surprising sense of compassion compelled me, I let my fingers do some walking. First, I rang my friend Leon Jones — a member of the contemporary Christian band, "The Resurrection" — and I asked a big favor. Miraculously, the band had a weekend free in December and quickly caught the spirit of my mercy mission to those behind bars.

Next, I dialed the prison in Florida. The officials decided to allow us to perform in the maximum-security area one night and a minimum-security area the next. As I let God lead, logistics fell into place. Yet, I worried about financing our planned Christmas visit.

Around Thanksgiving, I e-mailed my prayer partners for cover. I asked a few for dollars as well. We had already received several generous gifts, but the tally still fell $900 short of our airfare expense. By the next day, however, two prayer team members responded. One offered to donate frequent flyer miles. I got the second response late that night while sitting in my flannels and sipping a cup of tea at my computer. I couldn't believe what I found in my e-mail in box. Sheila Nicholson wrote:

> Dear Kim:
>   I can donate what you need. My husband was murdered in early 1998, and his murderer is in a maximum-security facility here in Indiana. Very recently, the Lord has been telling me that I need to forgive him for what he did. It is very difficult, but my heart has been very heavy regarding the forgiveness of those responsible for my husband's death. While your ministry will not directly affect the one I need to forgive, maybe this is a good first step. Perhaps you can even tell them that a victim who is trying to do the will of God helped make your trip possible.
> In His name,
> Sheila

Tears welled up as I marveled at this woman's compassion forged out of a delicate forgiveness. How else could she support ministry to men accused and convicted of the violence that had ended her husband's life and devastated hers?

The big day finally arrived and, despite the snow accumulation of a recent blizzard, we left Detroit and landed in Orlando on schedule. At the prison, we got clearance and guards ushered us to the maximum-security floor.

Our group — two women, three guys, and a junket of musical equipment — drew hard stares from the dour inmates. So, we quietly minded our own business en route to the designated concert cell. But within minutes, the amps bounced our music off concrete near and far. It was a "Holy Ghost party," to coin a phrase from a Resurrection song, and for the next ninety minutes we joyfully shared in word and music what God had done for us.

Two of the three guys in our group had done prison time, so their testimonies seemed especially relevant. My turn to speak came just before the last song, and I talked about forgiveness within the framework of Sheila's story.

"Tonight, there's a woman in Indiana who is praying for us," I explained. "This woman knows firsthand of the devastation of violence, and she also realizes that there is pain on both sides of the fence when an act of violence happens. She just wants you to know that she's trying to forgive the men who killed her husband and devastated her life. She cared enough about you guys to fund a large portion of this trip so we could do this concert."

The sound of silence hung thick for a few seconds as the reality of what I had just said settled into their minds. Then, smiles played on a few faces before applause washed over those words like a cleansing wave. The men stood and cheered Sheila's courage to forgive and to show compassion.

Yes, compassion's face comes with many different features. I've described its appearance in Mother Teresa, my mom, and Sheila Nicholson. Yet, it's the same Christ within that produces these unique expressions. From this point of view, the phrase, "Jesus looks good on you!" takes on a new meaning.

Chapter Three

I called this chapter "Compassion's Hall of Fame" because these women's stories have been such an inspiration to me personally. Notice a couple of common strands that run through each. One, these are everyday, run-of-the-mill, ordinary people (yes, even Mother Teresa). I chose them for that purpose. Sometimes I think we feel as though we have to start a nonprofit organization and solve the world hunger problem in order to fulfill God's desire for us to be compassionate. That couldn't be further from the truth. He just wants us to be available to touch the lives of the people He brings to us. That brings me to the second common strand.

As I look at each of their lives, it is evident that God first did a work within each of these women, the kind of hard, gut-wrenching work that most of us spend our lives avoiding like the plague. From that reshaping of their character, He blew into them the hope-giving compassion that comes only from Him. And from there, the natural outpouring of gratitude for what He did in their lives spilled out onto the people around them. It's not as if any of them had to work really hard to show compassion; in fact, Mom and Sheila probably feel a little uncomfortable being singled out, because they know that what has happened in their lives has been a God-thing more than anything else.

This is compassion's beauty. True compassion must flow from a river of gratitude that swells its banks with thankfulness over sins forgiven, hope restored, and wounds healed. Trying to be compassionate on our own will only leave us exhausted and overwhelmed. But if we give God the opportunity to clothe us with His *oiktirmos*, we will find He has quilted within us a patchwork heart that is willing to give itself away to others. When God pours His infinite never-ending love into our spiritual veins, we feel the beating of His merciful heart, and everything changes.

4

TUNING YOUR EARS

I live with two teenagers and a really cute eight-year-old. Thank you for feeling my pain. Anyway, whenever I agree to chauffeur this rowdy troupe, they fly out of the house ahead of me to start the car and tune the radio to their favorite bubble gum music station. As soon as I slide behind the wheel, this sound jam invisibly blocks our communication. The resulting isolation frees me to tune out the kids, tap my toe, and enjoy a strange sort of peace and quiet.

"Mom. Mom! MOM!" someone eventually hollers over the din of the speakers and engine. "We've been *talking* to you, and you're, like, *totally ignoring* us." Sometimes life gets so noisy and fast-paced that God must feel like my kids. He's trying to catch the attention of a person completely engrossed in a life on overdrive.

Yet, God designed us to be in relationship with Him, and — as with other important relationships — that takes plenty of unhurried time and attention. I've slowly prized that time, because I finally figured out that God is a great conversationalist. He listens well, concentrates on the nuances of the communication, speaks wise words, and never screams — even when justified by what He hears.

I, on the other hand, need to keep brushing up on my spiritual listening skills, which reminds me of the "Ear

Training" class I took as a college student. That semester I learned to recognize what each tone in the scale sounded like and how each one sounded in relationship to the scale's other tones. One day our professor told us that our final exam would include listening to a short piece in four-part harmony. He would then ask us to write all four parts on the staff.

Just listening to his announcement — much less listening to the ditty he planned to play during finals week — psyched me out. I almost dropped my music major because I felt so ill prepared to clearly hear the tones. But throughout the semester he patiently trained our ears, step-by-step. By the time that intimidating exam rolled around, I felt confident that I could accurately translate notes from his piano to my page. And I did!

In the same way, listening to God's voice takes practice. First Kings 19 tells the story of Elijah running for his life from evil Queen Jezebel. Never mind that God had just brought down fire from heaven, making toast out of the Baal prophets. Jezebel had let it be known that she planned on killing God's prophet, and so Elijah took off for anywhere Jezebel wasn't, which in this case happened to be the wilderness. Traveling forty days and forty nights, he finally found safe haven in a cave. Catching his breath while sitting alone in his dark, dusty hideaway, he began to cry out to God. At this point a violent wind came, then an earthquake, then a fire, yet Scripture says God was not in any of them. But after the fire, there was the sound of a gentle whisper. That was the voice of God speaking to Elijah (see verses 11-13).

Attuned to God's Voice

Voices are like fingerprints. No two are the same. But with people, as with God, you'll only be familiar with a voice when you hear it again and again. For instance, I've met every Tuesday during the past five years with an incredibly talented group. We bring together our unique gifts in spiritual leadership, music, drama, and visual arts to brainstorm creative programming for our Sunday church services. With this consistency, I can be working out of sight in another room, and I'll still recognize Syndie's voice. I've hung around her long enough to identify her bubbly laugh too — even her sneeze!

It reminds me of the Bible verse that speaks of recognizing the voice that matters most. Jesus says, "My sheep recognize my voice; I know them, and they follow me" (John 10:27, NLT).

Meditating on that Scripture, I picture a shepherd stepping out into the sunshine and meandering down the path to where his sheep graze. He greets them softly and runs his fingers over their woolly overcoats on his way to the next pasture. He is all they know. He cares for them, always making sure they have enough food and water. Because he sits on the nearby grass every day with a long crook, they trust him to protect them.

The Bible describes us as the sheep of God's pasture (Psalm 100:3). He created me (and you) to know Him, to live in His presence daily, and to listen to His voice. If I learn how to listen to God, no doubt I will simultaneously get a piece of His heart for needy people as well.

But how does that happen? How does God speak to me? How do I know that it's Him? How do I include Him in the comings and goings of my day? How do I talk to Him about my life? How do I hear Him calling me to show compassion? Is it possible to clearly hear from God without going to seminary?

Somehow, I had latched onto a warped idea. I figured that trained spiritual leaders had a connection that I never could, that they pointed their spiritual satellite dish in just the right direction. Meanwhile, mine haphazardly dangled off the side of the house. Though I wasn't set up for success, I would be satisfied to pick up any faint signal.

Of course, God speaks through the Bible, the circumstances of our lives, and trusted spiritual counselors. Yet, as I analyzed my relationship with Christ and considered my battery of questions, it suddenly didn't feel very personal. I felt spiritually closer to mere mortals, and that bothered me. I had something of a prayer life, but it was a ho-hum, stripped-down version.

"Sometimes it seems that our personal relationship with God is treated as no more than a mere arrangement or understanding that Jesus and His Father have about us," writes Dallas Willard. "Our personal relationship then only means that each believer has his or her own unique account in heaven, which allows them to draw on the merits of Christ to pay their sin bills."[1]

Stopping Long Enough to Listen

For too long, I related awkwardly toward God because I viewed Him as a spiritual pharmacist at the twenty-four-hour divine drugstore. When I struggled, I sidled up to that counter and begged for the magic pill. But I never popped in just to shoot the breeze. I could think of ten other people with whom I'd rather share special moments. But living this way made me feel wobbly, like driving through life with a flat tire.

As a teenager, I owned a purple Gremlin that gave me the same disturbing feeling one day. I loved that car. (I probably was the only one who loved that car.) As my first set of wheels, it instantly looked like my ticket to freedom and adventure. The ultra-compact dimensions made whipping quickly around corners a snap.

It was the "quickly" part that bugged my dad. I would barrel down our street, swing into the driveway, and stop inches short of the garage door. Dad would give me that look, the one that says, "Girl, you hit that garage door, and I'm going to be one unhappy camper." Thankfully I never hit the garage door, but I did manage to damage the car along the way.

Less than a year after the state granted me that coveted driver's license, I got my first flat tire driving down Forest Lane in Garland, Texas, en route to a friend's house. The car ahead had stopped to turn left, waiting for oncoming traffic to pass. A bit impatient, I decided to scoot by the car on the road's gravel shoulder.

My driving skills were still green, and I nearly drove into the ditch before bouncing back on the pavement. I thought it was a clean save until I heard the right front tire blow just after I finished passing. Alarmed, I slowed down — a little — and then decided it prudent to pull over and check out the problem.

That bald tire now looked flatter than a pancake, to use Texas vernacular. In those days, cell phones were a pipe dream, so I jumped back in and drove the five miles home. When the purple Gremlin shuddered off, my dad had already folded his newspaper to come out and stare at the trouble — not only a flat tire but a destroyed tire rim as well. The unhappy camper look distorted Dad's face as he inspected.

That afternoon, I learned to avoid driving on a flat tire for more reasons than one. Besides making a bad rubber situation worse, a blown tire makes for a dangerously rough ride. The unbalanced pressure in the front wheels upset the axle, and I found myself in a tug-of-war with the steering wheel just to stay between the correct two lines. The flat tire also cut my speed. I had to inch along instead of cruising.

I face similar encumbrances on a spiritual level by trying to run well without fully inflating my "prayer tire" along with the other "tires" — worship, service, study, fellowship.

Instead of helping me stay on track with God's will and noticing needy folks along the way, my flat prayer tire pulled me in all sorts of crazy directions. At worst, it proved dangerous — at best, distracting.

I needed to get this part of my life filled fast, so I studied the writings of my favorite prayer warriors. These saints refer to prayer as a special conversation. They didn't track the time they spent reading Scripture or petitioning God through prayer — thirty minutes in the morning, ten minutes at night. Rather, they tracked God's replies to their questions, petitions, and praise.

Meanwhile, I rushed into His throne room, zipped through my list of important stuff, and hightailed it out of there without so much as a "Howdy!" or "How are you?" Have you ever started a prayer by asking God what's on His heart — and stuck around for the answer?

Howard Macy writes: "To approach God with only an incessant stream of words is a filibuster, not prayer."[2] The dry quality of my life with God had more to do with my poorly developed spiritual ears than with Him being aloof. No surprise there! And that dryness directly affected the quality and quantity of compassion I showed to others.

Funny thing is, I performed spiritual disciplines religiously. I read the Scriptures, meditated, and even prayed. But I never really tuned my ears to hear God's voice in the middle of my busy life. It often felt as if my prayers hit the ceiling and fell down like mist destined to quickly evaporate without a trace. God seemed silent. Then it dawned on me that perhaps I needed to give Him a chance to say something.

Do you have a friend who only talks about her life, her problems? Every time she calls or visits, it's "me this" and "my that." "Oh, my arthritis is acting up today. Look at what I just bought. You're never going to believe what happened to me." Just when I think I've diverted her attention for a few minutes, she practically says, "How nice for you. Now, back to me."

The psalmist encourages, "Be still, and know that I am God" (Psalm 46:10). In recent years, I've learned to appreciate that if I do the first part, God will prove Himself in the second part. It's a matter of getting beyond the clamor and, like Elijah, tuning your ear to His still small voice.

"I always begin my prayer in silence, for it is in the silence of the heart that God speaks," wrote Mother Teresa, one of my compassion heroes. "God is the friend of silence — we need to listen to God because it's not what we say, but what He says to us and through us that matters."[3]

But plenty of things pull me from this stillness, not the least of which are time-related pressures. During a retreat for ministry couples, Henry Blackaby, noted author of *Experiencing God*, convicted me in this area.

"Do you ever have unhurried time with God?" he asked the group. (That question now hangs above my desk on an index card.) Was he kidding? I hadn't had unhurried anything for about ten years! Yet, he stressed the importance of unhurried time by adding that if God doesn't have access to you, all of the people in your life will suffer.

Jill Briscoe, one of my favorite authors and speakers, writes, "God wants all of us to be so in touch with him that we are tuned into heaven's wishes for earth."[4] Too often, I'm guilty of going about my business without giving a second thought to how compassion fits into my interactions that day.

Bob Keyes, an associate pastor at my home church in Texas, used to say that people do what they want to do. Given the time-starved lives so many of us lead, the "I don't have time" excuse hedges prayer out more than anything else. However, when a time crunch keeps you from your prayer closet, you can bet it will keep you from ministering with compassion to hurting people.

Chapter Four

Time to Be Compassionate

To thwart the work of compassion God wants to extend through you, the Evil One sprinkles doubts that can dampen your thinking. In my case, most of these doubts involve second-guessing God. Here's my hit parade of excuses — in order of popularity:

1. "Why, Lord, I'm sure I don't have enough time to do that and everything else that's already in my day."
2. "That person is sort of messy and could stress me out too much."
3. "Certainly that's not God speaking. He doesn't communicate with me this clearly or in this way."
4. "If I disciple her, then I won't be able to attend my Bible study. I'm sure you wouldn't want that. I need to be growing too."
5. "I don't know that person, Lord. What will she think if I just walk up, start talking, and offer to help?"
6. "I can't work at the soup kitchen. You know the inner city is too dangerous for someone like me."

The list can go on and on. But why wouldn't God — the same God who created dragonflies and flamingos, who started the redemption process, and keeps up with the tiniest details in everyone's life — find innovative ways to help us love one another with deep compassion? That's His nature. But I too often choose to mistrust the inner leading, to chalk it up to bad pizza or something else equally ridiculous.

Dallas Willard suggests that perhaps we don't hear God's voice because we don't expect to hear it. He adds: "Then again, perhaps we do not expect it because we know that we fully intend to run our lives on our own and have never seriously considered anything else. The voice of God would therefore be an unwelcome intrusion into our plans."[5]

Living a life of compassion doesn't legalistically obligate you to pick up every hitchhiker. You don't need to sign up for the local soup kitchen volunteer rotation to get compassion points with God. You simply must learn to listen to Him and be willing to respond when He does call. Perhaps it *will* involve a guy with his thumb out or a stainless steel ladle. It could also be as simple as baking cookies for a new neighbor on the block or volunteering at youth group to rub shoulders with a kid whose family life stinks. The apostle John explains that the Holy Spirit will tell you the things on the Father's heart: "The Holy Spirit is our teacher" (John 14:26, my paraphrase). Of the Spirit, Jill Briscoe writes: "If we will allow him to show us what to do in any given circumstance, he promises to take the things of God and clarify them for us."[6]

Does God have things to say to you? I can now say with great confidence, "Absolutely!" We can love confidently and well when we are sure God is moving us toward someone. If we will just take the time to sit at His feet and listen, He will speak, and every compassion endeavor will be marked by the words He breathes into our spirits. With that in mind, don't you think it's time to tune in?

5

OBEDIENCE

Like many young mothers, my sanity hung in the balance most precariously when my kids were knee-high or shorter. Both Lincoln and Brittany qualified when we moved to Michigan in 1989. They were squirts insatiably hungry for adventure. So, I scrambled to find an outlet for their energy and a place for me to quietly repose.

Griffin Park fit the bill with its grassy expanses and comfy benches. Instead of "Griffin Park," the entrance sign might as well have read "Garden of Eden" because it gave my kids and me a heavenly place to picnic, play, and relax.

One afternoon, another mom introduced herself and plopped down next to me on my favorite park bench. While I watched Brittany and Lincoln chase around out of the corner of my eye, we made small talk about the rigors of parenting. As we chatted, I discovered that she considered herself a single parent — even though she wore her wedding ring and still lived under the same roof as her husband. But this man left at the crack of dawn and didn't return until well past the dinner hour. Worse, when he dragged himself home from the office, he was torched from his high-energy, fast-paced day. All he wanted at that point was peace and quiet — and rounds of cold beer.

His chronic unavailability had forced her to manage

their household solo for years. She balanced the check-book, cooked, cleaned, contracted home repairs, and changed every diaper. Her son was now Linc's age (four), and already tapping her strength and getting on her last nerve with his 24/7 hyperactivity. Watching him play, I believed every word of her complaint.

As a relative newcomer to the community, she lacked friendship networks. She never attended church or clubs, which also limited her access to other informal support groups. It didn't help that her husband's job moved the family every couple of years. Her eyes frequently welled with the misery isolation brings.

I listened to this tale of woe for about an hour and tried encouraging her before packing up our bag of toys. Then, as I fished in my purse for the car keys, she asked about keeping in touch. I scratched my phone number down on an old grocery receipt and waved good-bye with a smile.

During the two-minute drive home, God began speaking to me about this forlorn woman. She needed a friend, but the pit in my stomach told me I didn't want to fill that spot. Involvement in her life would not be easy. Talk about needy! I had convinced myself that reaching out to her was a bad idea before I opened my car door. So I stepped out, slammed the door, and pretended that God hadn't ask me to help.

Two weeks later, I tagged the clothing my kids had out-grown and joined our subdivision in throwing an annual garage sale. Cars packed the streets and people clogged the sidewalks and lawns as they picked around for cheap treasures. I drank lemonade, caught up with neighbors, and tended the nickel-and-dime till at our table. Just before I went inside the house to make cheese sandwiches for lunch, I noticed a haggard-looking woman clutching the hand of a rambunctious kid trying to worm his way to free-dom. I couldn't believe my eyes. I had vowed to steer clear of the woman I met at the park, and here she was beelining for my porch!

Oh no! Now she knows where I live, I thought as my mind raced back to that day. Nevertheless, while I waited on customers browsing in their baseball caps and sundresses, our boys played together in the backyard, and we chatted. Her low-key desperation was almost palpable. But I felt little compassion. Rather, I recoiled in slow motion and wondered why God seemed to be singling me out as her primary friendship opportunity.

When she and her son at last left to check out wares at the next house, she reflected on the happy serendipity of meeting me at the park and again on my porch. I gulped when she mentioned it was a small world, and that we should develop this new friendship more formally. The world is sometimes a little too cozy.

That she showed up at my garage sale seemed more like a divine appointment than fluky coincidence. So why did my heart sink when she stepped on our property? I flat-out didn't want to keep this divine appointment. God had clearly placed this woman in my life, but I wanted her out.

Several days later, she dug up the number I had hastily scribbled in the park and she called. Could I meet her for lunch? I begged off, told her something about my crazy schedule, and promised to return her call when the dust settled. She politely accepted my excuses, and we hung up.

Before I had placed the phone in its cradle, I began feverishly brainstorming for bigger and better reasons to postpone this luncheon date indefinitely. Working in the creative arts business most of my life gave me great leeway in generating ideas. Boy, did they flow that afternoon! Better yet, they all sounded plausible.

In a few short minutes, I had given myself guilt-free permission to reject her lunch invitations as many times as it took for her to get the message in flashing neon. Surely she could latch onto someone else — someone with more free time, more common ground, more compassion.

Today I regret that decision because she is long gone without much love from me. I can't even remember her name, and I have since wept over the lost opportunity. Besides heartlessly stonewalling this lonely housewife, my selfish disobedience kept me from the beauty that belongs to every believer. It is the beauty of saying yes to God and giving yourself away for the sake of His kingdom.

Out of the Pew and Into the World

"True knowledge of God is born out of obedience," wrote John Calvin.[1] Truth is presented in the Scripture and we understand that truth by reading God's Word — ideally, voraciously! But Scripture's reality cannot be known until it is experienced. The Bible was given not just for the sake of knowledge, but also, and perhaps more importantly, for the purpose of transformation. Knowledge alone is simply not enough to transform our lives. We must personally experience what the Scriptures tell us about.

We all know Christians (let's keep this generic here!) who have gone to church all of their lives and have yet to experience true transformation through obedience. Every Sunday they are there with their smiles on ready to sing and "be fed." But judging by the rest of their week, we would be hard pressed to find any evidence of real obedience to God. They daily struggle with everything from overeating to substance abuse to explosive anger.

What does that say about God's power in our lives? We say He's the God of the impossible, but looking at our lives, those outside the faith would have trouble finding any living proof that He is doing the impossible.

Scripture tells us again and again that God is more

concerned about our hearts than He is about our behaviors, because He knows that our hearts drive our behaviors. So if we want to be able to give away our hearts to the people God brings into our lives, we must come to understand what's in them and allow God to reshape them so we can become more fully obedient to Him.

Clearly, choosing to express compassion when the chips are down requires obeying God at the deepest levels of your faith. He calls all believers to obey with consistency in the Great Commission (Matthew 28:19). He says "Go," and in Greek that verb more literally translates "as you are going." The implication here is that we will indeed agree to go.

Once you agree to interact with a needy world, it's not enough to respond by dabbing your eye with a clean white hankie. Obedience in this area often involves getting a little dirty in the daily grind.

In *A Heart Like His*, Beth Moore explains such an incident. While she waited in a busy airport to board her plane, she noticed an elderly man in a wheelchair parked close to the gate. He wore wrinkled clothing, and his long hair hung in a matted mane. As she observed the disheveled fellow, God called her to brush out those greasy tangles. This idea at first struck her as preposterous, even revolting. But the longer she sat there, the more she squirmed, until she left her seat to timidly approach the stooped man.

"Sir? Excuse me, sir?" she said quietly, discreetly. "May I please have the honor of brushing your hair?" He was a little hard of hearing and asked her to speak up. She soon felt forced to shout her question. Newspapers lowered and conversations paused when he finally heard her.

With wide eyes, he accepted, and Beth quickly fished a brush out of his worn bag to begin gently pulling apart the snarls. As she patiently worked from the crown of his scalp to the base of his scrawny neck, she noticed the tears running down his cheeks and staining his shirt. He then haltingly explained that he had been sick for some time and was flying to reunite with his wife after several years apart. He wanted to look nice when he got off the plane but had no one to help him get dressed, much less brush his hair. Earlier he had prayed to somehow arrive cleaned up.[2]

I typically think of obediently sharing God's compassion in one-on-one situations. But Jill Briscoe explains how God stirred her compassion for a group. Though a baby Christian at the time, she cared deeply for teens and wanted to share the good news with as many of them as possible. So, with boldness, she entered a dance hall where about a thousand teenagers were hanging out. Stepping onto the floor felt so intimidating and scary, but she obeyed God's call to go.

"I stood outside praying for the courage to go in," she recalls. "The courage never came, so I went in without it and found myself talking to the manager." To her amazement, he agreed to her request for ten minutes at the microphone during an intermission.

Compassion, coupled with faith-filled obedience, gave her the platform she needed to share something about God's love. Stepping down from the stage, she felt simultaneously shaken and elated. It seemed that for the first time in her life she had walked on water without sinking.[3] Have you ever been called to such radical obedience?

"You are my disciples if you *keep obeying* my teachings," Jesus said (John 8:31, my paraphrase). "Then you will know the truth, and the truth will set you free" (verse 32). Growing up, I always figured verse 32 referred to freedom from sin through Christ. That might work except for that verse 31.

"If you keep obeying my teachings, you will know the truth." Hmmmmm. Now, I understand that freedom from sin means greater freedom to obey God. But knowledge alone won't expand the borders of my heart or yours. I've been a churchgoer all of my life. Sitting in the pew and learning about obedience didn't change me much. It was inviting Jesus to step into my shoes and walk with me that did it. I had the knowledge, I had the capability — I just needed to move!

This truth reminds me of Kailee Sosnowski's dance premiere. We asked her to join other teens at our church in creating a "human video" — a cross between mime and dance — for an upcoming Sunday service. She's already a youth group leader, already a girl living the lyrics of the Chris Rice song we picked, "The Face of Christ." In it, Rice sings about showing God's compassion to others. Without any dance lessons under her belt, Kailee balked. But we eventually convinced her to accept the role.

Saturday quickly rolled around, and we met to choreograph. When Kailee arrived, she immediately announced that she needed everyone's patience because she wasn't really a dancer. Yet by the end of the rehearsal, she and the other young women moved with perfect synchronicity. The human video had morphed from a spaghetti of arms and legs into lovely disintegrating loops of energetic movement. The coleader and I began cheering and clapping because Kailee twirled in the middle of those dancing girls, and she stepped on cue with power and grace. We could not tell the difference between her and the others.

"Kailee is a dancer, and she just proved it!" I shouted to the group as the music faded. A shy grin crept across her face. Kailee has what it takes — the body type, the aesthetic mind-set, and the passion to create great dance. She just didn't know it until she practiced.

In terms of showing compassion, you receive a new identity and capability the moment you accept Christ. But do you recognize that you've got what it takes? Or, like Kailee, do you still need to get out there and dance?

Chapter Five

We Go Because of Who We Are

Neil T. Anderson has written many books about a believer's freedom and new identity in Christ. *Victory Over the Darkness* and *The Bondage Breaker* have impacted my life tremendously because they emphasize that God's estimation of a person is the truest estimation. Just look at these many Scriptures that describe who we are and what we possess because of our relationship with Christ:

- I am the salt and light of the earth (Matthew 5:13-14).
- I am God's child (John 1:12).
- I am a branch of the true vine, a channel of His life (John 15:5).
- I am Christ's friend (John 15:15).
- I have been chosen and appointed to bear fruit (John 15:16).
- I am a personal witness of Christ (Acts 1:8).
- I have been justified (Romans 5:1).
- I am free forever from condemnation (Romans 8:1-2).
- I am assured that all things work together for good (Romans 8:28).
- I am free from any condemning charges against me (Romans 8:31-34).
- I cannot be separated from the love of God (Romans 8:35-39).
- I am God's temple (1 Corinthians 3:16).
- I am God's coworker (2 Corinthians 6:1).
- I am united with the Lord, and I am one spirit with Him (1 Corinthians 6:17).
- I have been bought with a price. I belong to God (1 Corinthians 6:19-20).

- I am a member of Christ's body (1 Corinthians 12:27).
- I have been established, anointed, and sealed by God (2 Corinthians 1:21-22).
- I am a minister of reconciliation for God (2 Corinthians 5:17-21).
- I am a saint (Ephesians 1:1).
- I have been adopted as God's child (Ephesians 1:5).
- I am seated with Christ in the heavenly realm (Ephesians 2:6).
- I am God's workmanship (Ephesians 2:10).
- I have direct access to God through Jesus (Ephesians 2:18).
- I may approach God with freedom and confidence (Ephesians 3:12).
- I am confident that the good work that God has begun in me will be perfected (Philippians 1:6).
- I can do all things through Christ who strengthens me (Philippians 4:13).
- I have been redeemed and forgiven of all my sins (Colossians 1:14).
- I am complete in Christ (Colossians 2:10).
- I am hidden with Christ in God (Colossians 3:3).
- I have not been given a spirit of fear but of power, love, and a sound mind (2 Timothy 1:7).
- I can find grace and mercy to help in times of need (Hebrews 4:16).
- I am born of God and the evil one cannot touch me (1 John 5:18).[4]

For too long, I felt as insecure about my spiritual assets and abilities as Kailee felt about her physical ones. But embracing the truth about who I am in Christ has made all the difference in how I respond to God in obedience. With

His grace, confidence, strength, and freedom, I can befriend people like the woman I met in the park or someone like Lucia Capichioni.

Lucia is a lovely woman with incredible passion and *joie de vivre.* After we moved to Michigan, we eventually settled in a house on Adams Street next door to Lucia. But we soon learned that despite her natural buoyancy and optimism, emotional junk cluttered her head and heart. Ultimately, we watched her lose a successful business career, her house, and—at times—her mind.

The first red flag popped up on Christmas morning 1996. As my family and I laughed while digging out from the piles of colorful wrapping paper littering our living room, the phone rang. Lucia sobbed that her family had just been standing on her porch. We gathered that it was no happy holiday surprise. Instead of taking their coats and breaking out the gingerbread cookies, Lucia slunk into the farthest recesses of her home and breathed very quietly for the next twenty minutes.

Part of her recovery from depression involved severing ties with her family because their association evidently hampered her progress too much. Lucia took her therapist's directive seriously. She secretly relocated to Plymouth and bought a house on Adams. So, she understandably felt stalked when assorted family members pounded on her door unannounced and uninvited.

We tried alleviating her hysteria by listening and offering words of encouragement. But as in most situations that call for compassion, the bottom line involved being there for Lucia. We acted. Despite her swollen eyes and stuffy Rudolph-red nose, we invited her to celebrate Christmas over lunch at Eric's parents' house. Later, hours after she stopped hyperventilating from terror, Eric and I shared our faith. We explained that Jesus is a bridge over troubled waters, that He alone could see her through.

Lucia accepted Christ as her personal Savior that Christmas, and we appreciated that gift almost as much as she. Until late March, she built on her faith decision by studying the Bible with me. But that time of nurturing ended when her mounting bills forced her to sell her house.

We saw less and less of her then because, aside from leaving the neighborhood, she now spent about half of her time in North Carolina trying to land film work. Aspiring actors typically face tough times, but hers seemed extra bumpy. Though overqualified, she'd take menial jobs. Then, her boss would inevitably fire her anyway because her stress seeped into her work and ruined her productivity.

By the time she bottomed out, Lucia knew how cold a car can get at 3 a.m. in January—when the shelter's waiting list is a mile long. Sleeping in the freezing, unsafe conditions of the backseat only added to her restless unhappiness.

That season finally ended when some of her newfound church friends patiently supported her recovery to the point that she could rent a furnished apartment in Charlotte, North Carolina. Shortly thereafter, she heard God calling her to social work—to serving homeless people with compassion and empathy.

Recently, Lucia asked me to be a reference on her application to Gordon-Conwell Seminary, where she intends to get a master's degree in urban ministries. I viewed her note to our family as the ripe fruit of a seed planted out of obedience to God on a crisp Christmas Day years ago:

Dear Loved Ones:

The Lord has revealed to me that it is time for me to go to school to learn how to serve Christ. My pastor and an elder at church have prayed with me and agree that this is what my next step should be.

Certainly you will be rejoicing too for you have seen His work in my life and you carried the weight of so much of the pain. Thank you! You have been beautiful blessings!

As my walk continues and I realize more and more how important community is, I'm so sorry I didn't realize how beautiful your family's love is and your Jesus-like example. I had everything living next door to you and your family and wish I had known at the time how to love you in return. Know that you put a smile on my face just thinking about you. I love you!

Enthusiastically for Christ,
Lucia Capicchioni

Obedience-driven compassion tends to reproduce itself, and Lucia is living proof. Her personal mission statement reads: "My mission is to serve Christ by building apartment-style transitional housing developments throughout the United States without government funding, and to encourage the Body of Christ by providing awareness of the plight of the homeless through public speaking, fundraising, and marketing, bridging the gap between those who have and those who need." Sign me up! I want to give toward that cause.

"The greater the obedience, the greater the discipline, the greater the faith, the fuller and more complete the allegiance to our precious Lord — the more does the heart expand to receive more and more of Jesus," writes Alan Redpath.[5]

What would happen in your home, neighborhood, community, and country if you obeyed God in loving the unlovely? If you do the work of "going," of embracing radical obedience and unconditional love, God will do the inner work that translates into miraculously compassionate behavior. This type of sold-out willingness to accept faith adventures may take you around the block a few times. But you can press on in His strength.

Oswald Chambers once wrote, "Go, and don't stop going!"[6] I say the same to you!

6

COMPASSION
SQUELCHERS

I had just asked Hunter to grab his backpack as I reached to turn off the Today show. "Look, Mom, that building has a hole in it." I glanced up just in time to see what looked like a commercial jet crash into the second tower of the World Trade Center. The day — September 11, 2001. It's a moment that will be etched in my mind as long as I live. Likewise, many of us who are at least middle-aged retain a freeze frame of where they were when they got word of President John F. Kennedy's assassination. I do, though I was just a girl at that time. I also vividly recall the Kitty Genovese murder on March 13, 1964 — though for different reasons.

Kitty who? At three in the morning, this young woman was on her way home from work in Queens, New York, when a man attacked her with a knife as she walked from her car to her apartment. She screamed for help, and both she and her assailant expected someone to come to her aid. The man fled. But when the streets remained silent, he returned — not once, but twice more, to stab her to death.

During this intermittent half-hour assault, Kitty continued yelling and struggling to reach her door. She died in front of her apartment building, despite the thirty-eight witnesses the police investigation turned up. Many of those people recognized Kitty or knew her, yet her cries fell on deaf ears.

Shortly after the tragedy, our pastor stood in the pulpit of our church and shared Kitty's plight. I sat transfixed in the wooden pew, squished against my mom to fight off spine-tingling chills. None of the witnesses had even called the police! Like my pastor, the media picked up this horror story and stirred plenty of folks to think more deeply about character and moral responsibility.

After that Sunday, I thought more about the future too — more than girls my age usually do. Would somebody terrible visit my neighborhood? Would people in my town peek through drawn shades, unmoved to act on my behalf? Still, the story eventually died, just like Kitty. And nothing really changed with all that talk.

As a society, we're still fighting fear when it comes to being good Samaritans. When was the last time you stopped to help someone broken down on the side of the road? As I whip around a stalled car, I usually remind myself that it is in no way safe to stop. There's some truth to that. But putting up rigid defenses in the name of practicality may keep you from doing God's will in the name of compassion. Many times I have found myself in places of great danger and God has protected me. So, how do I automatically decide whether one situation is safe and others are not?

To find a more loving way of doing life, I return to Jesus' well-known parable recorded in Luke 10:25-37. Jesus told this story of the Good Samaritan to offer us a role model, and it's no accident that He used a Samaritan — someone whom the Jews disdained. After all, the Samaritans existed as a haunting reminder of Israel's sin as a nation — they were a product of intermarriages with people who worshiped false gods.

However, pain is a great shaper of compassion. When the Samaritan spotted the beaten Jew in the ditch, perhaps he instantly identified with the man's low position. Most likely he had been on the other side of hatred and jeers long enough to know that things aren't always as they appear. Ethnicity is like skin color, only skin deep. It means nothing more — and nothing less. Yet, the Jewish priest and the Levite, the equivalent to our modern-day pastors, both chose to avoid contact with this man so desperate for a helping hand.

No doubt, compassion squelchers were the same then as they are now. To develop into a believer with a patchwork heart, recognizing these squelchers and overcoming them becomes paramount. Here's a closer look at each of the culprits: fear, prejudice, time, complacency, and selfishness.

Squelcher #1: Fear

Not surprisingly, the most notorious compassion squelcher is fear, because in some way it drives the other squelchers. I may fear sharing time with someone else for fear of losing it for myself. I fear discarding prejudices because it may draw me closer to someone different from me. Who doesn't fear losing control or stepping out of the comfort zone of complacency? Perhaps even selfishness stems from a fear that if I don't take care of number one, no one else can or will.

Fear stems from many sources, but certainly not from God. Paul tells us, "God did not give us a spirit of timidity, but a spirit of power, of love and of self-discipline" (2 Timothy 1:7). If God has not given us a spirit of fear, then who has? Satan, of course. When fear wells up, Satan can quickly drown compassionate responses and immobilize believers from doing God's will.

By the way, the Bible also uses the word "fear" when it talks about a right relationship with God. For instance, the psalmist writes, "The fear of the LORD is the beginning of wisdom" (Psalm 111:10). But in this context, fear is more accurately defined as respect and awe. This fear inspires believers to follow God's will versus running from it.

But if Satan speaks fear into your heart, you may experience the real deal — a panicky, overwhelming terror. No wonder that response often prompts creative excuses for avoiding God's leading. In this way, fear sabotages countless would-be attempts to show God's compassion to broken people.

Through trial and error, I have learned that keeping in close touch with God and setting healthy limits often dispels the fear I have of loving kamikaze-type people. Instead of running scared, facing my fear and building appropriate boundaries can keep me in service for Christ with compassion.

Had I this insight twenty years ago, maybe I would still be in relationship with Donnie. Though he had a strong physical presence, something about this man's bearing readily conveyed that he was timid, unhappy, and even disturbed. His shoulders always slumped, and during the two years I knew him, he never laughed. It turns out that Donnie struggled at a very deep level with homosexuality.

I met him when he enrolled for private piano lessons during Eric's seminary years. From the start, Donnie seemed more interested in making a friend than learning an instrument. He even tried buying my friendship by bringing gifts to every lesson. And when I introduced him to Eric, hoping that a strong male role model might be therapeutic, Donnie started giving gifts to him as well.

Neither of us expected or appreciated these unsolicited gifts, but we feared hurting his feelings by rejecting them. Such a response, we learned, made Donnie feel rebuffed, causing him to become extremely upset and to accuse us of being phony, unfaithful friends.

Looking back, I see how fear caused us to tolerate this kind of manipulation. Dealing with an emotionally unstable person like Donnie, someone who often called late at night threatening to end it all, caused us to walk on eggshells. At some point, worrying about Donnie turned to fearing him. We had repeatedly encouraged him to get professional counseling, but he regularly brushed off that advice. His condition worsened and his three A.M. suicide calls picked up. We even visualized him showing up on our doorstep to take himself out and take us out with him.

Instead of drawing stricter boundaries, we prevented him from encroaching on our peace by cutting him off altogether. Fear caused us to make this snap decision. But I'm not sure it was the right one, the most compassionate one, the one God wanted us to make. In our young adulthood, we didn't have many coping skills. Now, after years of ministering to folks with emotional brokenness, we know that people in pain behave in very uneven ways. We were never bold enough to get past our fear and talk plainly to Donnie about consequences for behavior we found worrisome.

Today, instead of abandoning Donnie, we would more likely ask God if we should live with the tension these kinds of relationships create. If God is calling us to stick close to such people, He will enable us too. The apostle Paul reminds us that God will not give us more than we can handle, but will make a way for us to bear up under the weight (1 Corinthians 10:13). There have been times when I have felt stretched to the max as I have completed my compassion assignments, but I have never fallen under the weight of them, and God has used them to increase my faith and build my inner world in ways that are deeply satisfying.

Squelcher #2: Prejudice

I have met very few people who acknowledge their prejudice, much less identify it as a compassion squelcher. Instead, most prefer to consider themselves open and tolerant when it comes to accepting others. Yet prejudice continues to surround the most problematic race and class issues. Prejudice also taints the relationship mainstream people have with those on the fringes — the poor, the homeless, prisoners. Even in the church, where scriptural teaching underscores that there is neither Greek nor Jew, but that we are all one in Christ (see Galatians 3:28), tolerance of diversity is not fully embraced.

Because prejudice often lives in subtle forms, it's easy to brush it off — to believe that you harbor prejudice against no one. If that's true, great. If not, the first step to beating this compassion buster involves recognizing it. To find out where you stand, take this simple quiz. You might have prejudices if you:

- use the words "those people" when referring to anyone from a different ethnic or social background
- purposely avoid eye contact with homeless people when you see them
- become fearful passing a person of another ethnic background on the street
- distrust a particular people group
- get the creeps associating with someone less fortunate
- don't have a friend from a different ethnic background

How did you fare? If you answered yes to even one of those statements, you may need to reconsider the ways this compassion squelcher is interfering with your ability to live as a person with a patchwork heart.

Like fear, prejudice can be overcome with faith, hope, and love. Consider Nan Walker. She sensed God asking her to reach out to a prisoner — despite her many fears about befriending folks behind bars. But Scripture calls believers to remember the forgotten with compassion — as if you were shoulder-to-shoulder with them in their straits.

Hebrews 13:3 tells us to "remember those in prison as if you were their fellow prisoners." Yet many people fear being manipulated or even pursued when that inmate is released or escapes. Fears aside, welcoming crooked or otherwise violent folks with blood on their hands into your life presents a great challenge of balancing prudence and wisdom with compassion.

Meet Desmond today, the prisoner with whom Nan eventually corresponded, and you'd never guess his life's story. Just putting a face and a name to the word "prisoner" can dispel some of the fear to make room for the second chances compassion affords. He's an affable, caring, forty-something man with a ready smile and an energetic spark in his eye. He's the kind of guy you feel like you've known all your life — now that he's been paroled on good behavior from the Kentucky facility where he served a segment of his original twenty-five-year sentence.

But before he walked free and clean — physically and spiritually — this convict lived each day in the loneliness of depression and despondence. He eventually longed to end his life and began planning the particulars. Then, while flipping through radio stations in his cell on an evening shortly before the secretly scheduled suicide, he paused long enough to hear Dr. Dobson's "Focus on the Family" program with guest speaker Carol Kent.

For the first time since his lockdown, he felt hope — the strong hope found in Christ alone. When the program ended, he quickly jotted down the Focus address and wrote a letter requesting Carol's address. He wanted to thank her for delivering a message that encouraged him to go on living.

Not long after Carol received Desmond's letter, her church friend Nan offered to volunteer in the Kent ministry office. While going through the mail in Carol's office, they reread Desmond's letter. That's when Nan sensed God moving her past her prejudice in order to encourage Desmond in his walk with Christ. As she and Desmond corresponded over the years, he sensed a call to ministry as well. Other prisoners had noticed a change in his life and, eventually, he enrolled in a seminary program offered at the prison. He recently walked out of the pen as a free man with a mind transformed by God — something encouraged by two women who put prejudices about prisoners aside to show compassion.

Squelcher #3: Time

In the twenty-first century, time is money. Hence, the late twentieth-century proliferation of time management systems. But even without a direct relationship to the dollar, millions of Americans want more mileage for their minute. That explains why the words "Franklin Covey" sound like music to the masses. Yours truly is one of those people — a woman guilty of wishing for more hours each day to do more. Without getting an extra second, I still push myself to the point of exhaustion to get a desired result.

From the moment I rise in the morning, I'm checking off items on a long "to do" list. Still, my kitchen only stays clean when nobody's home. Perhaps my family could move out for a week to give me the sweet relief of walking in and seeing every dish in place, every countertop wiped off. Instead, I chronically feel the urge to grab the dish soap and a towel. The laundry area? Ditto! Like dirty dishes, dirty laundry is never done. Between housekeeping, working, and driving the children all over creation to music lessons, gymnastics, play practice, and Cub Scouts I often live in the land of the time-starved.

In *The Sacred Romance*, Brent Curtis and John

Eldredge make a valid point by stating that sometimes our identity is synonymous with activity. Ouch! Is it any wonder that time qualifies as a compassion squelcher? If I keep busy to be important, why would I have time to stop and serve someone who may be on a slow track — or stuck completely?

Scripture says my identity comes from abiding in Christ (see John 15), not from abiding in activity. That means getting a grip on what I can and can't do, and learning to set the appropriate boundaries. It means saying no to some things so I can say yes to the most important things, the things God cares about. It means allowing God to craft each day alongside of me, knowing that He does not intend for me to be exhausted by daily tasks. It means believing in His promises and trusting that He is a kind, benevolent Father looking out for my best interests.

However, when I slip and shut God out of my schedule, the excuses often sound so spiritual: *Why, if I did that, then I wouldn't have as much time for my family or my own spiritual growth.* But God has a way of taking obedience and maximizing it in unimaginable ways. I didn't know this as a teenager.

Back then, in the 1970s, I participated in a dynamic church youth group that visited shopping malls, parks, and other high school student hangouts every week to share the good news. One balmy summer evening, in a park close to church, we found a cluster of kids our age just standing around shooting the breeze. They immediately coded us as church teens thanks to our conservative look — no shorts and no pot. But they listened intently as we shared our stories, and I couldn't help but notice the girl with big blonde hair and a great mid-summer Texas tan.

Jan was cute, spunky, and curious. She asked lots of questions. She also asked for my phone number, thanked me, and said she'd see me Sunday. To my surprise, Jan

Chapter Six

appeared as promised as I stood in the church lobby trading weekend news with my friends. Everyone's head turned to catch a glimpse of the new girl as she marched up to me.

"I told you I'd show up," she proudly stated. Not only did she show up, she hung out with us after the service. When she departed with a wave, she promised to return. We soon gathered that Jan was a woman of her word. For several weeks she arrived promptly and immediately found me in the crowd. I seemed to be her home base in the youth group, and rightfully so. After all, I had invited her in the first place.

A month of Sundays quickly passed, and Jan then asked to join my friends and me outside of youth group activities. My stomach sunk as her question hung in the air. Suddenly Jan went from being the nice new girl to a leech. I liked her well enough, but now she was beginning to want more of my time, and I wasn't sure I liked that.

In my three years of park outreach, Jan was the only person who had actually come to church more than once, the only one that demanded a greater time investment. Without discipleship experience, I figured that helping this budding Christian to grow would take untold hours — hours I didn't want to spend with her.

The fear of making that kind of time commitment soon squelched my compassion, and my interaction with Jan became more strained as the weeks flew by. Here was a girl who needed to know more about Jesus and could have used my support, but I found myself wanting to pull away rather than come alongside. In retrospect, I wish I had talked to my youth pastor or parents about how I was feeling and how to proceed. Sadly, I didn't. Jan eventually got the message and stopped coming to church.

Time still represents a powerful compassion buster. But since then, I've learned to shift the burden of discipleship from my shoulders to God's. If I have time to share the truth with someone, it's that person's choice to grasp it — or not. Whatever time I can afford to spend discipling will be time well spent. But I couldn't see Jan from that perspective. Instead, I felt solely responsible for helping her succeed as a Christian — and only if I spent lots of time with her.

If you're a time-starved person looking for direction on what to add and what to delete in your Day Timer, consider these questions:

- What is your role in the relationship? Are you realistically the only one who could spend time discipling that person?
- If you feel God calling you to spend time with a needy person, are you willing to live with the tension? Are you willing to let Him rearrange your day?
- Can you trust that there is a profound connection between showing compassion and growing your faith?
- Have you surrendered your ownership of time and accepted that it's really God's time?

The psalmist wrote, "Teach us to number our days aright, that we may gain a heart of wisdom" (Psalm 90:12). Are you spending your time in wise ways, ways that glorify God?

Squelcher #4: Complacency

Humans are most definitely creatures of habit who for the most part live to create and maintain stability. Because showing compassion often causes believers to act outside of their comfort zone, it's no wonder complacency represents another potent compassion squelcher. It takes energy, time, ideas, and in some cases money to lovingly help needy people. In comparison, sitting in an easy chair to read or do a crossword puzzle looks good.

Here again, avoiding compassion stimulates creative excuses in the average believer: *My life is already full enough; I don't need one more thing to do. I work really hard; I deserve a break today. How much difference am I going to be able to make in someone's life anyway? I'm sure there are plenty of other people volunteering who are more gifted than I am.*

While there might be a kernel of truth in those statements, without consulting God, that type of decision-making strategy comes down to this maxim: "If it feels good, do it." If showing compassion becomes taxing or expensive or heartbreaking, don't do it. The problem with that line is that God often calls His people directly into difficult situations with broken people in need of genuine compassion and love.

Opportunities to show compassion often knock at my door when I feel least prepared to answer with a resounding, "Yes! I'd love to help." Typically, when I feel most drained, when I just can't wait to get home and retreat, someone at our church will approach five minutes before our family packs into the car.

"Can we talk?" he or she will say hopefully.

No! is my first reaction. I'd like to say, "I've got plenty of problems of my own. Plus, I'm beat." But I know I can't pick and choose ripe ministry moments like I pick bananas at the grocery store. Deep down I understand that my response to God and to that person shouldn't be based on convenience, but obedience. Walking away from those situations is almost always a mistake, lost chances to be used by God for good.

Still, I remember one conference where I thought, *Lord, being totally available is just out of my reach today.* Having just finished leading an intense session, complacency seemed like an OK indulgence — especially since I was stationed in the auditorium only to help another speaker with the video presentation. As she moved through her introduction, I got comfortable in my chair by the back door. I was missing only one thing — hot, leaded coffee.

Five minutes before I needed to be tracking with her main points, I slipped out to the lobby to find a Styrofoam cup and the urn, hoping with every step that it had not been tapped out. That's when a straggler to the presentation showed up.

No wonder she arrived a few minutes late. With advancing multiple sclerosis, she struggled to walk and tottered with nearly every step. To make matters worse, she practically burst into tears shortly after we gave each other a smile and the standard, "Good morning." The woman soon confessed that, though interested in the topic being addressed inside, she really just needed to talk with someone.

At first, I hoped that a strong cup of coffee would help her snap out of it so I could return to my post in the quiet darkness of the room. Nothing doing. She launched into the story of why she felt that leaving her husband was the only option at this point since they argued about money, child rearing, communication — all the biggies. She had no hope and no help at the moment. Meanwhile, my wristwatch seemed to tick like a time bomb, and I became aware of how puffy-eyed and sleepy I still was.

Complacency awaited just inside the door, but compassion seemed to involve listening to this woman and encouraging her. So, I found a last-minute audio-visual sub and followed God's urging. By the time we finished talking thirty minutes later, she thanked me for keeping her from taking the easy way out. As she hobbled into the auditorium at last, I silently thanked her for keeping me from taking the easy way out too.

Chapter Six

Squelcher #5: Selfishness

Sometimes pure selfishness squelches compassion. Anyone struggling to move into a place of showing more compassion probably has a zillion stories to illustrate how successfully selfishness will derail these good intentions — along with so many other Godlike leanings.

The same holds true for me. Each month I find myself at the airport taking off for destinations in the United States and around the world. Airport life is like another reality as people from all walks of life and a variety of nationalities mingle. So I people-watch and enjoy anonymity. However, remaining nameless is a little tougher when you sit shoulder-to-shoulder in cramped conditions for hours with fellow passengers.

During one flight from New York's LaGuardia airport to Detroit after a busy weekend of giving concerts, I longed for some downtime — some "me" time. I collapsed in my seat and planned to chill out without saying much of anything to anybody. Then I spotted who would be filling the other three seats in my row — a young mom with two young children in tow.

This woman was desperately trying to get to the seats by clutching the baby to her chest with one arm and using the other one to drag her three-year-old down the narrow aisle. Besides her son, an exceedingly large bag rolled along behind the bulky blanket draped over her shoulder. Just watching the procession made me feel tired. By the looks of it, my nap would be anything but undisturbed. Yet ten minutes later, she had gotten herself and her kids quiet and secured — ready for takeoff. Whew.

Within minutes we were airborne, and that's when the peace broke. The baby must have had ear pain, and nothing could stop the flood of tears and screams. The mother tried everything that I would have tried, but nothing seemed to help. Then, the three-year-old decided he wanted off the plane and was trying to get out into the aisle. He began screaming too, which only added insult to injury for the baby.

A small voice inside (and we all know who that was) told me to help this distressed mom. Just an extra pair of hands might have been helpful. I sat there for a minute and the excuses began to pour through my mind. *She will probably be offended if I ask to help. Her kids would probably balk at a stranger's assistance.* You name it, I thought it. Ultimately, this compassion squelcher kept me frozen for the entire flight.

Driving home from the airport, I couldn't help but mull over in my mind that whole situation. Why had it been so hard for me to just say, "Can I help you with anything?" As I was thinking it through, God slipped into the conversation. He reminded me that I had never really even asked Him what He wanted for that situation. I was tired and I didn't want to respond, so I just ignored Him. I missed what God had for me and so did that tired mother. I regret that missed moment, and with God's help I hope to not miss many more.

Ultimately I lose as much as the person God asks me to serve when I choose to let any of these compassion busters ruin a love opportunity. The patchwork heart God is cultivating in me loses its rich texture and vibrancy when I choose not to share it with others. Each time I squelch compassion's fire, a piece of my heart is lost, wasted. We must make the commitment to ourselves and to God to rid ourselves of whatever weighs us down, so that we might fully express His love in the opportunities He presents.

Faith
Adventures

"One small step for man, one giant leap for mankind." As that poetic phrase issued from our kitchen television set, I sat glued to my chair watching the live coverage of Neil Armstrong's extraordinary moon walk. Until now, that chalky soil hadn't been touched since the time of Creation. As Armstrong held a curiously starched-looking American flag to make our country's conquest official, my career questions were answered at the tender age of eight.

NASA, here I come! I mused to myself. I aimed to be an astronaut, to fearlessly surf the universe — the final frontier. Back then, I embraced high-stakes adventure and had busily plotted my trip to Pluto before passing a single aeronautical engineering class. All things were possible with a little imagination, perseverance, and faith.

However, as the years passed, my itch to quest took a practical turn as I juggled more down-to-earth demands that involved school, marriage, children, work, and ministry. And so it was that I started settling down before I ever lifted off. There would be no moon walking for me unless it happened on a dance floor. But whenever I start counting on the status quo, God usually upsets my apple cart.

It tipped soon after a moving truck rattled down our

street and parked next door. Out sprung couches, lamp shades, boxes marked FRAGILE, and two girls about my daughter's age. The girls immediately powwowed at our house, and the already high decibel level inside escalated appreciably with the fits of preteen giggles.

Later that afternoon, I met their mother — a perky, streetwise, twenty-seven-year-old — and we hit it off as famously as our daughters had. Niki soon shared her hard knocks, but assured me that her top priority now involved building a better family life for her children. She considered this goal within reach. After all, she had a new-and-improved husband and house. She figured her future would follow suit.

Though she smiled when we met, Niki now tells me that taking up residence next to a minister's family never thrilled her. But, she quickly sized us up and allowed us into her world when she discovered we did not act holier-than-thou.

For a precious few weeks, we watched her happily put down roots. Then, life turned upside down for this newcomer. When she returned from running errands one day, her husband had almost turned the key in the moving van's ignition. He had packed hastily and roared away before anyone could change his mind. In minutes, the only thing left of him was a faint plume of black exhaust.

Niki immediately slid into a financial dilemma because the couple had purchased their home based on a double income, and now she was forced to make the monthly mortgage payment alone. To her credit, she took steps to solve this pressing problem by landing a higher-wage job at a nearby auto assembly plant.

That job covered her costs and minimized her commute, but it also presented some significant drawbacks. For one, working on the assembly line taxed her physically. Worse, she worked the second shift, which made home seem like a revolving door. Minutes after her girls walked in from school, she needed to head off to work. When she finished her shift and returned around midnight, they had long since gone to bed. Nevertheless, Niki stuck it out because the company fueled her hope for a first-shift transfer.

Then, within the space of thirty days, Niki changed dramatically. The divorce, her unexpected financial pressures, and the ongoing isolation from her children began taking a toll. Though she made it to work every afternoon, she withdrew when at home, living in a fog of depression. Her girls — ages seven and eleven — suffered greatly from this physical and emotional absence, yet Niki stubbornly refused to hire a baby-sitter.

Everything came to a head when Stevie, the oldest daughter, pounded on our door in tears. Her dad had threatened to take Niki to court in order to gain full custody of the girls, which would mean moving to the country and seeing their mother just once a week. My heart went out to Stevie, and I vowed to help. This kid had spent so much time at our place already that she seemed like one of my own brood.

"Stevie, what would your dad say if we told him that you and your sister could spend the night with us when your mom works?" I asked. "Do you think he would back off of the custody thing?"

With a little hope in her heart, she bounded back across the lawn to find out. Meanwhile, I rang Eric at his office to get his reaction. He agreed to let the girls stay with us. Stevie showed up the next day with a toothy smile. Her parents gave the plan a green light. For the next nine months, Stevie and Destinee joined us for dinner and camped upstairs five nights a week.

I'm hardly polishing my halo over this act of compassion. Truth is, my fingers itched to call social services and report this mother for leaving her children alone at night to fend for themselves. I longed to stand on my front porch with my hands on my hips, clucking at Niki's neglect. Instead of showing compassion and extending assistance, I would just as soon have judged her and let the screen door slam behind me.

Do you have anyone like Niki in your life? Is someone on your block or in your Bible study overwhelmed by life and taking it out on her kids? Your knee-jerk reaction may resemble mine because so often poor choices cause these dilemmas. Like me, you may think, *Geez, lady. Get it together!*

Until recently, I never considered that people like Niki may have tried to do just that and, so far, their efforts have failed. But when all this chaos broke out just paces away, God's voice miraculously drowned out my own. It must be another example of His amazing grace because I knew my response boiled down to obedience or disobedience.

"You can either stand there and judge her," God whispered, "or you can help. I hope you'll choose to help."

Help we did. As expected, Stevie and her younger sister Destinee easily blended into the comings and goings of our family and seemed happier for the care. Niki, on the other hand, continued flailing and finally bottomed out. A repetitive stress injury gave her a legitimate break from her job thanks to a medical leave, and she used that time to rethink her priorities. She appreciated that we had poured lots of time and love — not to mention groceries — into her children. And, ultimately, our show of compassion opened the door for Eric and me to share our faith in Jesus with her. It softened Niki's heart.

To our delight, she found a personal relationship with Christ and started attending our church almost immediately after our first conversation about God. Her life took a 180-degree turn, and she picked up with her girls where she had left off nearly a year earlier. When she finally got back in the driver's seat as a full-time parent, we counted this blessing again and again. She still suffered some depression-related symptoms, but her uphill climb to better health was well underway.

A Call to Further Adventure

One beautiful summer morning, as I sat on my front porch visiting with God, He moved my heart to compassion again. Ken Gire's devotional book *Moments with the Savior* lay open on my lap to the story about the demon-possessed man whom Jesus healed (Mark 5:1-20).

I tend to focus on the healing, but Ken wrote most about the man's suffering. What was it like to be so estranged? How did he try to fit in? He asks the reader to pray for children oppressed by harsh realities. I couldn't help but think of the girls next door. As I prayed for them that morning, God called me to help them by helping their mother.

Help their mother? I bolted upright in my chair. What was God talking about? I had been helping their mother practically since the second I met her. But it seemed that God wanted me to give more — to disciple her weekly. Teaching a depressed baby Christian was not part of my agenda for the next few months, so I resisted.

"Lord, I can't possibly take on this assignment," I prayed with a rising sense of panic. "You know how much I have on my plate now. I'm traveling all over the place. I'm on staff at church. I lead a very busy life of ministry. When I'm home, I need to devote myself to my children and husband. I'm sure you'll understand if I bow out of this one."

The next morning, I met with God on my porch again and read the next chapter in *Moments with the Savior.* This time, Ken commented on John 8:1-11, the account of the woman caught in adultery. Niki was no adulterer. But the description of this woman so beaten down by life reminded me of her. My eyes misted as I read this excerpt:

> She turns to go her way, leaving behind her a life of sin. There are no tears as she leaves. Years later there will be. At odd moments during the day: when she looks at her children asleep in their beds; when she waves good-bye to her husband as he walks to work in the morning. A marriage she never would have had . . . a family she never would have had . . . a life she never would have had — were it not for the Lord who stood up for her when others wanted to stone her, who stooped to pick her up and send her on her way, forgiven.[1]

I knew God wanted something better for Niki. I knew she needed someone to disciple her with compassion. But, again, I tried to avoid stepping into that time-consuming role.

"Lord, this is just impossible," I responded with my hands folded, my eyes squeezed shut, and my brow furrowed. "I'm already overextended for the next fifteen years! How could I possibly give an afternoon every week to this woman? Hey, remember how you've been encouraging me to manage my time better? I'm making a go of that, but this looks like two steps backward."

The clock ticked as I perched on the porch feigning deaf ears.

For the third consecutive morning, I retreated to the porch to open my Bible and my devotional book. Before becoming completely engrossed, I noticed Niki popping out of her house — ponytail bouncing in the breeze and lit cigarette in hand. She waved good morning, then jumped in her car and drove off.

It gave me pause. Then, when I opened *Moments with the Savior*, bold print spelled out that day's entry title: "Who Is My Neighbor?" I laughed and cried simultaneously as I read about the Good Samaritan, because I sensed that God wasn't going to let me go. The clincher hit when I read the closing prayer:

Dear Jesus, . . . Forgive me, Lord, for being so concerned about my other commitments that I am unconcerned about my commitment to others. Help me to realize that so much of true ministry is not what I schedule but what comes as an intrusion to my schedule.

Keep my schedule flexible enough, Lord, so that when my path comes across someone in need, I would be quick to change my plans in preference to yours.

Give me a heart of compassion that I may love my neighbor the way the Good Samaritan loved his. Give me eyes that do not look away and feet that do not turn to the other side of the road.

Who is my neighbor, Lord?

Is it the woman next door, stripped of her happiness, black and blue from a bad marriage, wishing she were dead?

Deliver me from stillborn emotions, which look at those on the roadside with a tear in my eye but without the least intention of helping them. Amen.[2]

This time, I bowed my head not just to mull over the possibility of discipling Niki, but to surrender. Despite my overbooked planner, I decided to trust Him with the logistics of the relationship. That very day, I sent a card over to her house with these words penned inside: "God's been speaking to me about you, Niki. He has some things He wants to tell you. If you are interested, I can help you learn to hear His voice."

She called the next morning and asked when I wanted to meet. Forty-eight hours later, we were sitting in a restaurant talking about life and faith — a weekly habit we still keep. And God kept His end of the bargain by giving me compassion where there was no compassion and creating space in my calendar where there was no space. Given the six-day Creation story, this shouldn't surprise me. But it still does.

Niki would argue that she benefits the most from our time together. However, I get the privilege of watching her take faith steps so willingly. She thinks her prayers sound so simple. But I get to reassure her that they are exactly what heaven wants to hear. She's walking the talk and — by discipling her — so am I.

Still, it disturbs me that I didn't initially jump at the chance to go on a faith adventure with a literal neighbor like Niki. How could I walk with God for more than thirty years and still not trust Him to help me reach out with compassion? I've long studied the Word about that and even earned a minor in biblical studies. Yet, somehow the information didn't translate into anything transformational.

I equated more knowledge with more faith. But it doesn't work that way. Remember the Pharisees? Jesus had run-ins with them left, right, and center. Even though these temple hotshots knew all that there was to know about the Scriptures, it never sank in deep enough to make their character more like God's. They knew the letter of the law and completely missed the spirit.

"A disciple is a learner, but not in the academic setting of a schoolroom, rather at the worksite of a craftsman," writes Eugene Peterson. "We do not acquire information about God, but skills in faith."[3]

What do you do with what you know? Reminiscing

together over lunch one day, Niki told me that just two things made her listen to what Eric and I had to say about God. First, instead of judging her, we pitched in. We cared for her children when she was working the second shift and grappling with messy personal problems. She noticed that we walked the talk.

When she paused to take another bite of her sandwich, I wondered what reason number two could be. She daintily wiped her mouth to speak one word — *laughter*. It regularly percolated out of our house and stirred her curiosity. Notice that our biblical knowledge didn't even rank! Instead, our compassion and willingness to invest in her life weighed as heavy as gold on the scales of her heart.

From Fear to Faith

"Faith develops out of the most difficult aspects of our existence, not the easiest," writes Eugene Peterson.[4] That really flies in the face of my longing for a peaceful, stress-free life. It's a little unsettling at best. At worst, it can keep you tossing and turning all night long.

I admit to a few sleepless nights when I mulled over accepting other faith adventures from God. After all, His assignments are generally God-sized, not Kim-sized. Job experienced similar apprehensions and, indeed, he lost family members, friends, property, and cash. As the Old Testament patriarch himself confessed, "What I feared has come upon me; what I dreaded has happened to me" (Job 3:25).

Recognizing the possibility of those fears becoming reality is natural. Allowing them to shrink your heart is a different story.

For years, I obsessively worried about putting our kids through college. Ministry staff positions rarely pull down plump salaries. I also recall giving lip service to

God's protection, but I could hardly get a moment's rest the night before boarding a plane to speak or sing — in His name, nonetheless.

Fear had a death grip on me, choking out my ability to make faith-based choices. I had lived in fear so long that it was comfortable and seemed normal. I sensed that I was like everyone else struggling to do life on planet Earth. The only problem with that line of thinking is that I was comparing myself to others and not to the truth in God's Word. The apostle Paul wrote, "God did not given us a spirit of timidity (fear), but a spirit of power, of love and of self-discipline" (2 Timothy 1:7). God drew me to grapple with that verse and the fear-related issues in my own mind. And thanks to some serious housecleaning on His part, I am experiencing a freedom that has completely reshaped the way I extend myself to others.

Fear can cause you to extend yourself only to the degree to which you feel confident and comfortable. But make no mistake. That perspective lacks true faith. It turns God into a pussycat — lovable, but reduced to hanging around the house and making very few demands. No genuine faith adventures come from this kind of living.

Remember that throughout the Scriptures God calls His people to look past their fears and to blindly trust Him. If you feel stretched, consider Moses. God called him and a couple million Hebrews to believe in Him as a deliverer — even if it meant parting the Red Sea and closing it up in time to drown the pursuing Egyptian chariots.

"Faith is a way of looking at what is seen and understanding it in a new sense," challenges Frederick Buechner. "Faith is a way of looking at what there is to be seen in the world and in ourselves and hoping, trusting, believing against all evidence to the contrary that beneath the surface we see there is vastly more that we cannot see."[5]

After eleven years in the pastorate, Eric and I have listened to the stories of hundreds of hurting people. If taken at face value, we would wonder about God's plans because we can see only so much of the picture.

King David must have felt that way often, if the Psalms are any indication. Consider Psalm 69, where he cried out, "Save me, O God, for the waters have come up to my neck. I sink in the miry depths, where there is no foothold. I have come into the deep waters; the floods engulf me. I am worn out calling for help; my throat is parched. My eyes fail, looking for my God" (verses 1-3). Yet, despite his feelings of abandonment and discouragement, he acknowledged the rest of the picture (God's love and goodness, verses 13,16) and thanked God in advance for His deliverance (verses 30-36).

God will never leave you or forsake you. He's a high-stakes adventurer, and He calls you to follow His lead, wherever the path. The same Moses who was so fearful of standing before Pharoah early in his ministry years later wrote this to his successor, Joshua: "Be strong and courageous, for you must go with this people into the land that the LORD swore to their forefathers to give them. . . . The LORD himself goes before you and will be with you" (Deuteronomy 31:7-8).

Eugene Petersen writes: "Discipleship is not a contract in which if we break our part of the agreement he is free to break his; it is a covenant in which he establishes the conditions and guarantees the results. Our life with God is a sure thing."[6]

Finally, if you embrace God — even in tough circumstances, if you choose to walk the talk, He promises to transform your mind (Romans 12:1-2). You will see the world and the people in it from a heavenly perspective, not a human one, and that makes all the difference in developing a patchwork heart. Suddenly, you'll find something to appreciate in that pesky coworker. Or, you'll notice somebody everyone else thinks is a nobody.

Patchwork hearts can have a domino effect. After God gave me the compassion to reach out to Niki, she responded by reaching her world in the same way. Like many new believers, she immediately sought to share her faith with her entirely unchurched family. Her mother, Cassie, and her sister, Tiffany, knew nothing of God's love. Niki's first attempts to share the good news by explaining her testimony fell on deaf ears. Their indifference frustrated her, but I kept encouraging her to just keep on living the Christian life.

Eight months had passed when Tiffany called Niki out of the blue to say that she had noticed a big change in Niki's life. That telephone conversation evolved into a weekly Bible study group that Niki led exclusively for her family. She was a little anxious about stepping into leadership, but she used a book already creased and highlighted from her own study and, as her mentor, I made myself available to field tough questions or thorny issues.

Every week, Niki invited her family members to accept Christ. They always explained that they weren't ready, or that they needed more time. Then, several days after one of those weekly Bible studies, it happened. Tiffany called Niki to accept Christ. And Niki phoned me to report the wonderful news.

Tiffany evidently made up her mind after listening to a Christian band. Band members shared their testimonies in between sets, and that caught her attention. When she heard what God had done in their lives, the basics she was learning at her sister's Bible study started clicking.

I attended the next Bible study at Niki's place to hear Tiffany share her first faith adventure with the rest of her family and to encourage her spiritual growth. Trudging the short distance through the snow back to my house, gratitude filled me when I spotted the empty white Adirondack chair I had sat in just two summers before. That's where, during several special dappled mornings, I wrestled long with God over leading a Bible study with Niki. I paused on the third step and looked up at the huge moon looming over Michigan and then past it into the starry heavens.

"Thank You for giving me the privilege of being a part of Niki's life," I prayed. "I'm so glad that You insisted and persisted, convincing me that we could do this together. If it hadn't been for You, I would have missed this moment."

Being a Grace-Giver

Mention the word *Titanic*, and most folks can tell you about the notorious "unsinkable" ship that now rests on the Atlantic's floor. Despite the tragedy, I fell in love with the most recent film version — the 1997 blockbuster starring Kate Winslet and Leonardo DiCaprio — because the costumes, cinematography, and romance all told a captivating story of good and evil, gain and loss.

But as I strolled out of the theater, a disturbing thought pounded between my temples. A massive, rock-solid iceberg lurked under the waves, ready to slice open the ship's hull. Had the captain simply respected the potential beneath the surface, the crew and every passenger would have reached New York City safely and on time.

Like the captain on the *Titanic* that fateful night, I too can miss seeing the greater part of what lies beneath. After all, in navigating troubled interpersonal waters with a compassionate heart — instead of calculating caution — I have shipwrecked on the jagged icebergs of ingratitude, dishonesty, impatience, selfishness, and despair.

In the midst of unknown oceans, God promises His grace to serve as my compass and shield. When I take the helm of my life with that grace in my heart, He either charts my course around unseen dangers or miraculously holds me together when I crash into life's hard, hidden obstacles.

I always hope for the first-case scenario, but I've slowly learned to see through His eyes in the case of the second. This ability reminds me of Italian Renaissance painter, poet, architect, and sculptor Michelangelo Buonarroti. When asked how he transformed a roughshod chunk of stone into a polished form, he supposedly replied, "I saw the angel in the marble, and I just chiseled until I set him free."

He saw the angel when no one else could because he looked past the apparent. God's grace can give you the same uncanny ability. Instead of letting rocky circumstances and crusty exteriors blind you to compassion, you can choose to see the God-given dignity and potential every needy person presents.

Being a grace-giver is, of course, easier said than done. Like me, you probably have a mental file thick with hurtful experiences that threaten to close your heart to future "tough" cases. I still remember the first time a fellow student betrayed me after I befriended her in the spirit of compassion. Jackie and I attended the same high school, and I soon noticed how much she struggled academically and socially. She lacked self-confidence, and many thoughtless classmates added to her misery by relentlessly mocking her.

I decided to reach out by inviting her to sit with my girl-friends and me at lunch. Later, I included her in our after-school social circle, and I chastised those immature high school guys whenever they started calling her names. As we spent time together, I enjoyed Jackie's company more and more. Underneath her downcast glance, a funny, bright young woman hid.

The year before I graduated, we brainstormed to give her a comprehensive makeover. I encouraged her to try a new hairstyle, exchange her glasses for contact lenses, and acquire some more fashionable clothes. Her once shrunken confidence swelled with each change, along with her sense of self-respect. In less than a year, Jackie had morphed into a different person — inside and out. Even the once heartlessly cruel guys started treating her better.

I left for college the next fall, and she stayed to finish her senior year. But we kept in touch by writing letters and hanging out when I returned home for breaks. Four years later, when I graduated from college, Jackie called with some terrific news. She was engaged! Would I be a bridesmaid?

To watch her transform from an ugly duckling into a radiant bride thrilled me, and I was doubly blessed to be a featured part of her special day. Despite Eric's and my extensive summer travel schedule that year, I managed to arrange time off the weekend of Jackie's wedding.

Three months before the big day, the phone rang again. I could tell that something was up the minute Jackie said "hello." She stuttered and peppered her jumbled conversation with a dry, nervous cough.

"This is really difficult," she finally said. "So, I'm just going to say it. I've decided not to have you be a bridesmaid in my wedding."

Jackie's call devastated me for weeks. I wasn't her closest friend at that point, but I had contributed a lot to her life. Being abruptly excommunicated from her bridal party puzzled me. The facts surrounding her decision surfaced months later when I discovered that her maid of honor — a mutual friend of ours — harbored a grudge against me. I was unaware of the misunderstanding at the time, so I could hardly take steps to resolve it.

The maid of honor and I ironed everything out eventually, but for a long time it bothered me that Jackie had allowed someone else to call the shots at her wedding. Frankly, it still stings that Jackie never looked over her shoulder at how I forged a friendship with her when no one else would. Why couldn't she find it in her heart to honestly discuss the issue before rescinding the brides-maid invitation?

After that three-ring circus, I vowed to keep my heart in its rightful place — safely tucked in the cavity of my own life. Temporarily losing that friendship shaped the way I looked at every other relationship. I trusted others less and protected myself more. Giving away a piece of my heart had cost me too much, and I didn't have the grace to get past my bitterness to forgive.

I'm not alone in this conundrum. Plenty of well-meaning Christians learn early on to guard their hearts in the name of pain management. However, for a believer, that presents a serious problem. It goes against the grain of what God does and calls us to do — to be grace-givers at all times, in all seasons.

"In this world you will have trouble. But take heart! I have overcome the world," says Jesus (John 16:33). His words take on new meaning when we realize that pain is a part of life, and that God has historically manifested many miracles in the midst of it. John 11:1-44 chronicles Lazarus's death and the mourning that followed until Jesus returned and restored his friend's life. Acts 16:16-34 documents Paul and Silas sitting chained in the Philippian jail until a heaven-sent earthquake freed them. Instead of fleeing, they stayed and saved the life of their jailer.

To get my hands on that kind of grace, I was forced to give God my bitterness over Jackie's ingratitude. I had to forgive — and get used to forgiving — because it's a big part of showing genuine compassion.

Embracing Forgiveness

For inspiration in this area, you need look no further than the late Corrie ten Boom. Her best-selling book *The Hiding Place* chronicles how her family helped hide and protect

Jewish families in Holland during World War II. The ten Booms paid an exorbitantly high price for their compassion. Corrie's father and sister both died in prison camps after being discovered by the Nazis. Corrie was imprisoned too, but she survived and later traveled all over the world to share her testimony.

In *Tramp for the Lord*, she recalls a speaking engagement she reluctantly accepted in Germany just two years after the war. When the American troops released her from the Ravensbruck death camp, she had vowed to flee Germany and never again set foot on its tainted soil. Yet she heard God calling, and she chose to obey.

After Corrie finished her message about forgiveness, a well-dressed gentleman came to the front of the auditorium. She immediately recognized him as one of the Ravensbruck guards, and her blood ran cold. He had been particularly mean to her and her sister, Betsie. Now, he thrust his hand out in greeting.

"A fine message, Fraulein!" he said. "How good it is to know that, as you say, all our sins are at the bottom of the sea!" Corrie fumbled in her purse to avoid shaking his hand and mumbled her agreement.

"You mentioned Ravensbruck in your talk," the ex-guard continued. "I was a guard there. But since that time, I have become a Christian. I know that God has forgiven me for the cruel things I did there, but I would like to hear it from your lips as well. Fraulein, will you forgive me?" Once again he reached out his hand in friendship.

Corrie's heart skipped a beat. She couldn't bring herself to shake this man's extended hand, much less forgive him for his torturous, murderous behavior. He and his cronies had devastated her family. Scenes of her life at that death camp flashed through her mind and a World War III-like struggle mounted within. When she couldn't reach out, she reached up to heaven for help.

"Jesus, help me!" she frantically prayed. "I can lift my hand. I can do that much. You supply the feeling."

When her hand mechanically clasped the man's hand, a most miraculous thing happened. God showed up! Corrie immediately sensed His healing presence when she touched her persecutor with compassion and grace.

"I forgive you, brother!" she cried. "With all my heart."[1]

Facing the Truth

In addition to embracing forgiveness, facing the truth about yourself and others makes a sturdy stepping-stone to grace-filled compassion. The simple maxim, "The truth hurts," often resonates when you're trying to love needy people. Yet truth is often the sharpest tool God can use in performing the necessary soul surgery.

How hard is it to look at the truth and address it? We spent last Christmas at my in-laws' home. One of the kids channel-surfed television stations and landed on a courtroom scene from the film *A Few Good Men* as we chatted. Instantly, the guys in the room zeroed in on the TV and hunkered down.

Tom Cruise plays a prosecuting attorney bent on extracting the truth about a Marine-base murder from a commanding officer played by Jack Nicholson. Strictly by-the-book officers dressed in pressed military uniforms pack the courtroom in support of their colleague.

Challenging the commander again and again, with no admission of guilt, in desperation the attorney pauses and states: "I want the truth."

That line freeze-framed the courtroom—and my in-laws' living room as well! Finally, from their trancelike state, my husband and the other male family members watching the action leaned forward and curled their collective upper lips to snarl with Nicholson: "You can't handle the truth."

My sister-in-law and I turned to each with the "Now, that's scary!" look on our faces and then continued nibbling our pumpkin pie. But I admit that I've heard that line plenty of times over the years. It's the line the Evil One whispers every time I try to be honest. He doesn't want me to look hard at the difficult areas of my life or someone else's, because doing so can awaken my heart to hearing God's truth and heeding His will. It gives me hope and strength to journey through life in a radically different way.

Finding the boldness to face the truth is an important step in developing a patchwork heart. But the obstacles of stubbornness, self-centeredness, and pride kept me from appreciating this. For instance, during summer 1980, I traveled with my college's publicity team. We performed concerts across the country and recruited high school students as we toured.

Though I wouldn't have spent three of my precious "college" summers any other way, the first time on the road proved challenging. My personality mixed like oil and vinegar with that of tour director Steve Winget, and we often hotly disagreed. By June, I believed that he had a vendetta against me.

When we stopped to sing somewhere in Florida, Steve asked if I had my music portfolio in hand. Annoyed to find that I had once again left it in the van, he launched into a lecture about keeping it with me at all times. Something about his tone of voice grated on my nerves, and I gave him a piece of my mind on the spot. That conversation fell so far short of how God expects us to interact that I almost bought a bus ticket for home that night.

I managed to find my portfolio and warm up with the rest of the group. But after the service, my situation rapidly went from bad to worse when I discovered that I was staying at the same address as Steve and his wife, Cheryl.

As Steve got ready for bed, Cheryl gently pulled me

aside to talk in the kitchen. Sensing that she had suspended her judgment, I shared my side of the story and complained that Steve had hurt my feelings with his wrath.

Without meaning to take sides, Cheryl tactfully reminded me that Steve had asked me to keep my music handy from day one. I had agreed to do just that at our first rehearsal, well before we ever hit the road. After all, ours was a team of vocalists who had memorized the music. I, on the other hand, accompanied them on the piano. Without every note down pat, I needed to have sheet music available — at a moment's notice.

Being confronted with the truth made me squirm, but it also forced me to take responsibility. I needed to be ready to rehearse whenever the group got a spare moment. Cheryl ended our conversation with a smart question. Could I put myself in Steve's shoes?

I reconsidered Steve's leadership role on our team. He had shouldered a heavy responsibility by taking ten students on tour for ten weeks. Since he needed to present a brief talk at the end of each concert, and rarely gave the same message twice, he faced the added pressure of preparing in a van filled with noisy laughter and multiple conversations. When the van broke down or other problems cropped up, guess who needed to solve them? Cheryl's question lingered. If I were in charge of the tour, and one person kept leaving her music in the van, would I fume a little?

Those honest reflections stirred some compassion in my rigid heart. It helped that Steve soon walked in on our conversation and apologized for getting angry. But I had a genuine change of heart before hearing, "I am sorry, Kim." Sure enough, compassion made the bridge from my choppy circumstances to God's calm sea of grace.

Besides seeing my circumstances differently, facing the truth changed how I viewed myself. I confessed that I had made a mistake, and somehow that confession made it easier to be a grace-giver to Steve. I also realized that I would have probably acted similarly if placed in his position of leadership. And, after working through the truth of this conflict, the summer brightened and the many ensuing positive experiences influenced me to enter ministry full time.

Learning Patience

Becoming a grace-giver requires embracing forgiveness and facing the truth, but one stepping-stone remains— patience. I am not a patient person. As a girl, sitting still through dinner felt like waiting for Christmas to roll around when the calendar read January. Much to my mother's dismay, I would unconsciously tap my foot on the floor under the table. She considered this behavior rude and would shoot me the "Are-you-doing-that-again" look.

If the look failed to quiet my twitching, she would discreetly reach under the table to clutch my knee. That stopped me, but not for long. Instead, I ate barely enough to sustain life and then wiggled until excused early to roam my neighborhood with the other kids.

I never outgrew that impatience. I'm a woman on a mission, and I practically dare anyone to try to get me off track. If I'm not careful, I could easily buy into the slogan, "Lead, follow, or get out of the way." But a patchwork heart, with compassion enough to give grace, takes abiding patience. Interestingly enough, *compassion* and *patience* stem from the same Latin root word, *pati. Pati* means "to suffer," so compassion means "to suffer with."

Henri Nouwen writes,

> The compassionate life could best be described as a life patiently lived with others. If we then ask about the way of the compassionate life — about the discipline of compassion — patience is the

answer. If we cannot be patient, we cannot be compatient. If we ourselves are unable to suffer, we cannot suffer with others. If we lack the strength to carry the burden of our own lives, we cannot accept the burden of our neighbors. Patience is the hard but fruitful discipline of the disciple of the compassionate Lord.[2]

Remember the words of the apostle Paul quoted earlier in this book: "Therefore, as God's chosen people, holy and dearly loved, clothe yourselves with compassion, kindness, humility, gentleness and patience" (Colossians 3:12).

Paul encourages believers to "put on" compassion, as one would put on sandals or a cloak. The idea is that of receiving it as a gift from God — good news indeed for compassion-challenged folks like me. God does the work of compassion first *in* me, then *through* me. Once placed within, it is my responsibility to share that compassion with others.

"Compassion is a divine gift and not a result of systematic study or effort," Nouwen writes. "At a time when many programs are designed to help us become more sensitive, perceptive, and receptive, we need to be reminded continuously that compassion is not conquered but given, not the outcome of our hard work but the fruit of God's grace."[3]

I wonder what the outcome of the *Titanic*'s history would have been if the crew serving that fantastic ship had responded differently on that maiden voyage. What if they had taken the time to scrutinize the waters through which they sailed? What would have happened had they paid more attention to the iceberg warnings they received? I'm convinced that if they had known the danger, they would have certainly made every effort to avoid it completely. Knowing what to look for in those murky waters was critically important to the success of their journey.

The same is true as we move along compassion's pathway. So many times we will be called upon to see more than what is apparent — to see what *could* be, to envision unearthed potential when it's really, really hard to find. But God, who sees perfectly into each of our souls and knows what He desires for each life, can help us become grace-givers. He will enable us to give our hearts away in the most innovative and creative ways — if we can learn to be people of grace, seeing what He sees.

Leonardo da Vinci was one of history's most gifted innovators, a man truly ahead of his time. One of his mottoes was *saper verdere,* which means "knowing how to see." As a young man da Vinci studied the flight of birds. For hours and hours he watched in fields and recorded their movements in intricate drawings. Eventually he determined that it would be possible for man to make a flying machine, using the scientific principles of aviary flight. Considering that he made this discovery five hundred years before the first flight was ever attempted is amazing.

Only recently has the brilliance of da Vinci's drawings gained the notoriety due them. Now that we can actually video birds in flight, his drawings have proven to be highly accurate. Da Vinci trained his eye to see the subtle movements that the rest of us can detect only in slow-motion photography. The lesson for us? He took the time to learn.

Is it possible for us to *saper verdere* — to know how to see — when it comes to seeing what God sees and acting with compassion? Certainly. If we are but willing, God will help us to embrace forgiveness, face truth, and seek patience, the stepping-stones to a patchwork heart. Let us then commit our lives to the discipline of seeing what God sees, of choosing grace before all else. And then let us allow that knowledge to impact our actions so that we become true grace-givers.

9

LETTING GOD
ORCHESTRATE

A prominent businesswoman in our community recently lost her battle with cancer. And though friends and acquaintances suspected death at her door, they nevertheless appeared bewildered at her well-attended funeral. Though we knew this woman only casually, the loss hit home because our friend Michelle (Meesh) had worked with her, and because Eric was contacted to conduct the service.

Shortly after he got the call, Eric stopped in at the woman's workplace to check up on Meesh and to ask Fran Toney, the woman's boss, if she felt comfortable delivering the eulogy. After taking a seat in Fran's office — but before launching into eulogy guidelines — he quietly asked how she was doing.

Like Meesh, Fran struggled to concentrate on her work in the midst of ringing phones and swinging doors. She understood that folks simply wanted to express their condolences in a timely manner. But the deluge of emotionally loaded contacts was obviously taking its toll.

After briefly discussing funeral-related issues, Eric said his good-byes and headed back to the church office. As he shuffled papers on his desk, he noticed his black nylon bracelet with the white stitched acrostic. Just the day before, we had given everyone at church the black bracelets as a simple reminder to tell others — Friends, Relatives, Acquaintances, and Neighbors — that God loves them. The F.R.A.N. acrostic was now wrapped around his wrist as a timely reminder. A smile began to creep around the corners of his mouth. God has such a sense of humor. He was really going out of His way to tell Fran how much He cared about her!

The next day at the funeral Eric arrived a few minutes early so he could talk privately with Fran. Pulling her aside in the hallway he showed her his bracelet and explained that we had given them to the people of our church to remind them that their friends, relatives, acquaintances, and neighbors were all people who matter to God. He further explained that God wanted her to know that she was deeply loved and that her pain mattered to Him. Fran was deeply moved and put on the bracelet immediately. She wore it all that day and for several days afterward.

Later, Eric called Fran to invite her to a grief support group for some of the people he had met at the funeral. She jumped at the chance and began recruiting others! God has greatly used that support group setting to begin softening hearts.

Compassion moved Eric to visit Fran in the first place, which opened the door to a fantastic ministry opportunity. But we both credit the chain of events that led to the support group as a clear-cut case of staying flexible and letting God orchestrate. In this case, Eric got the idea for the F.R.A.N. bracelets and followed up by sharing them with our congregation and with folks like Fran herself. He sensed God calling him to give his bracelet to Fran, and that obedience caused a positive domino effect.

For a person who scurries from point to point with a planner safely tucked under her arm, the thought of allowing God to reorder her life on His whim makes me sweat.

I much prefer to live a day that ticks off on schedule from dawn to dusk. That way, I can control what's coming down the pike. No surprises, thank you very much!

However, in responding to God's leading, spontaneity must be the top consideration. If I stick my nose in my planner and glue one eye on my watch, who knows what I'll miss walking down the street? Will I notice that person God wants me to meet — much less minister to in His name? If I'm a slave to a set-in-stone routine, how many impossible ideas will I "waste time" entertaining?

I wonder if I'd see Jesus buzzing around with a pencil behind His ear and a planner in His hands if He lived next to our house on Adams Street. During his thirty-three years on earth, He went about his Father's business. Though that business didn't fit into neatly arranged slots, Scripture never indicates that He skipped breakfast to dash from village to village. He did what God told Him to do, and it was enough — not too much. He consistently showed up at the right place at the right time by letting God mess with His schedule.

Solomon once wrote, "Mortals make elaborate plans, but God has the last word. Put God in charge of your work, then what you've planned will take place" (Proverbs 16:3, MSG).

If you long to show God's compassion to the people in your world, allow Him to carve out time in your life according to the possibilities He sees — not just the ones you see. Inconveniences of every description — from a toothache to a longer line at the bank — can represent God reordering the events of your day to do His good thing. Living with this perspective will shake up your schedule and, at the same time, firm up your faith.

Willing to Let God Lead

Syndie and her husband, Jim, moved from California to Michigan so that Jim could attend seminary. During their settling-in process, they visited our church and decided to call it home. Syndie has a wonderful voice, and soon she joined one of the worship teams.

Eight months later, she began a period of intense soul-searching, sensing God was trying to transform a hurt that few folks knew about. People in those shoes often put their antennae up — consciously or unconsciously — to find one of God's patchwork hearts to hear the story and help.

She confided in me after church one Sunday. I couldn't begin to guess the nature of the hush-hush conversation she requested, but I agreed and we found a quiet room. I took that as the first miracle of many in Syndie's life, because at our church, quiet anything is uncommon.

"What's up?" I asked with a matter-of-fact smile and slightly arched eyebrows. Syndie stared at the linoleum, and I knew skeletons could be dancing out at any minute. She bit her lip and kept her emotions in check. Grasping the delicacy of the situation, I told her that her words would not shock or hurt me — that I wouldn't think any less of her for revealing a deep, dark secret. After so many years of counseling hurting men and women, Eric and I agreed with Solomon. There is nothing new under the sun (Ecclesiastes 1:9).

As it turns out, Syndie needed help to battle her weight. Delivering three children on the heels of one another would cause pounds to stick to any woman. But even before her babies, Syndie had struggled to eat in moderation and keep herself at a healthy body weight. She finally felt ready to explore the underlying issues that drove her to the fridge at midnight.

"Is it possible to sin with food?" she asked. I confirmed her hunch, and she admitted that overeating distracted her from satisfying her spiritual hunger — from pursuing a deeper relationship with God and others. It sounded like it was high time to book a "freedom appointment" for my new friend.

Our church hosts a soul-care ministry, and one of the counseling tools we use often is called a freedom appointment. Using material from Neil Anderson's "Freedom in Christ" counseling program, we help our members break the strongholds of sin — whatever their source. While a person's freedom appointment is confidential, Syndie has graciously given me permission to share her story here.

Perhaps Syndie was first inspired to change when, during their first Sunday service in Michigan a year prior, she heard Eric teach the principles in Anderson's book *Victory Over the Darkness.*

Eric defined the word stronghold and then explained that strongholds of sin can choke you spiritually and keep you from enjoying abundant life in Christ. He pointed out that habitual sin breaks everyone in one area or another. But if you allow God to reveal that brokenness, His healing power can transform your inner life.

People lined up in the aisles for prayer after that sermon. But instead of kneeling among them, Syndie just shared how thankful she felt about the soul-care ministry. Now less than a year later she in so many words was telling me that she should have left her seat that Sunday.

We met soon afterward for the freedom appointment. An hour into the meeting, I opened the section that addresses forgiveness. Syndie suddenly got bogged down in her responses. Earlier, she had disclosed hurts that related to an old boyfriend. She mentioned some infractions, but figured that at this late date not forgiving him was a forgone conclusion. Five minutes later, she lowered her head and whispered that she couldn't pray — that she couldn't continue.

I waited. And I furtively wondered how God could take my compassion for Syndie and give me insight on how to proceed. She nodded her head in agreement when I asked if my prayer partner Jen, who sat with us, could pray. As Jen prayed for Syndie, I prayed on a slightly different track. I wanted to identify the holdup. So, I asked for God's help and tried to remain relaxed and open.

Then, like sound floating from another room, I sensed God telling me to ask about her greatest sorrow. Based on our discussion thus far, I had no reason to probe this way. Seconds later, God unlocked hidden, graphic images. Syndie's sorrow flooded my mind.

When Jen finished praying, Syndie looked up at me. As our eyes met, I thanked her for her honesty up to that point. But could she tell me her greatest sorrow? Her shoulders slumped, and her face wrinkled as it does before tears flow.

"I slept with him," she stated flatly. That admission uncorked ten years of bottled pain. Though happily married to Jim, she never forgave her ex-boyfriend for the sin in which they both participated. Worse, she knew that God's plan for her life excluded premarital sex. Without an effective strategy to confess, forgive, and move on, she stuffed her shame out of reach — almost.

Learning more of Syndie's history explained her struggle with weight. Once her old boyfriend told her that he was going to fatten her up so that no one else would take her away from him. Syndie subconsciously allowed her ballooning figure to become her way of holding on to that relationship from an emotional standpoint. As I shared how she could find closure by turning to Christ rather than to second helpings, she has slowly learned to put food in its proper place — and the pounds are melting off. We've even nicknamed her "Slimdie" to encourage her progress.

If you bring a patchwork heart to each new day, God won't waste it. As you step into these often demanding situations, He's got tabs on the best plan. In Syndie's case, I caught on to His voice fairly quickly and was able to serve as a catalyst in her healing process. However, sometimes I wrongly assume that God's got laryngitis when He's just busy working underground. The key remains to be flexible enough to let Him orchestrate the outcome, to continue in compassion, and not to allow frustration or the desire for a "quick fix" to take over.

Willing to Wait

The first time I met Christina Davis in person, I realized that our tight connection during a prior telephone conversation was legitimate. We had effortlessly shot two hours with Ma Bell before either of us noticed the time. But sometimes rapport changes after formal introductions, and I prepared for a little letdown. To my delight, Christina turned out to be a fast friend — long-distance and face-to-face.

She first grabbed my attention through her book, *Totally Surrounded*, which recounts her faith adventure in the Philippines. Every page proved spellbinding, and I read her story of obedience and high-stakes missionary service in nearly one sitting. Clearly, God led Christina to the "X" that marked His spot for her. She brought entire jungle villages to a saving knowledge of Christ and returned to the States in the mid-1980s only because of volatile political unrest.

Packing up in such a hurry, she probably forgot a few personal items. But the dreams she had when the jumbo jet lifted off from that island stuck with her long after she landed stateside. Faces of Philippino orphans pervaded her thoughts with their pressing need for food, clothing, shelter, and God's love. Now thousands of miles from providing hands-on help, images of orphaned children on the streets of Manila — so young and unprotected — haunted her.

Christina's compassion for them grew year by year, and she envisioned one day returning to a town on the outskirts of Manila called Tagaytay. There, she planned to build an orphanage dedicated to sheltering Manila's forgotten homeless children and showing them God's love. She could even picture the future facility's layout — several small homes that could each comfortably house eight to ten children and the handpicked house parents. She also planned to build a hub for the houses, a large multipurpose area to stage recreational activities, classes, and Bible instruction. God had even given her a name for the place — Hope House.

Twelve years passed, and Christina married and started her own family. But she hadn't stopped praying about the children she left behind. She kept offering herself — her time and her every resource — to God for His use in getting the walls up and the roof on. Hearing nothing, she waited.

In 1998, Christina and a friend decided to return to Manila on a fact-finding mission. After two weeks of touring various facilities, starting an orphanage from scratch seemed more overwhelming than ever. At the same time, she leaned in that direction because none of the existing facilities fit her dream. Then, three days before the women departed, their guide tried curbing their discouragement.

"There is one more orphanage we will visit," he said. "It is in a place called Tagaytay." Christina could not believe her ears. What's more, as they approached the property, her heart fluttered to see a virtual carbon copy of the layout she had pictured in her mind.

"Welcome to the Hope House!" the orphanage's director shouted after Christina scrambled out of the car and up the path to the front doors where he stood with a smile. Shocked that the location, layout, and name mirrored her dream, she quizzed him for details. Soon, she learned that the founders purchased the original plot the very year God gave her the dream!

Furthermore, though the building projects wrapped up long ago, the director explained that the orphanage was facing a financial crisis that year. Christina pressed for the exact figure needed, calculated the current exchange rate in U.S. dollars, and realized that the money she had saved from her book sales equaled that need nearly to the penny.

This story of God's hand carrying out the dreams of His most compassionate servants sounds too good to be true. But God often seems too good to be true. Christina must have thought that, especially when she got another green light from Him soon after returning home. A couple summers later, teams of like-minded Americans traveled to the Tagaytay orphanage to build new housing units for increased capacity.[1]

Willing to Let Your Little Become Much

As the founder and CEO of the biggest miracle-making business in history, God knows how to work with impossible circumstances. For Him, the toughest part of pulling off a miracle involves finding enough folks to give Him a piece of their heart. He can work with that.

Frankly, my cup rarely overflows with compassion. But Matthew 17:20 explains that if you have faith the size of a mustard seed you can move mountains. God can take faith mixed with a little compassion and make it much. If you can embrace that truth, you can embrace the most remote possibilities of making a difference in the life of a needy person.

John Ortberg writes about just such a character. As a high school student, Toby wrote an essay about world hunger that won him a two-and-a-half week trip to Africa with a World Vision study tour. This unexpected adventure gave him a radical change of scenery short-term and an excellent learning experience long-term. The trip could have wrapped up on that note. Instead, an Ethiopian boy he met there at the last minute changed his life.

The child begged Toby for his T-shirt. As the teenager looked down at this boy with undeniably tattered, dirty clothes, compassion moved him to give the proverbial shirt off his back. However, just before tugging it over his head, he remembered that his luggage had already been stowed and would be out of reach until he arrived at his final destination almost a day later. The blisteringly hot African sun would burn his pale skin, and he doubted that the other airplane passengers would approve of him flying shirtless. Still, the needy stranger's request planted a seed in Toby's heart.

Once home, Toby organized a T-shirt drive. He persuaded local stores to put out bins for collecting the shirts and attracting media attention. When he emptied the bins, he found 10,000 T-shirts for Africa. Thanks to the campaign's overwhelming success, Toby now faced an unexpected problem. Shipping two tons of T-shirts to Africa would cost approximately $65,000!

Trusting God, he finally got hooked up with Supporters of Sub-Sahara Africa, an organization with a supplies shipment to that continent already in the works. The staff agreed to haul the T-shirts, but there was one catch. All of the shirts would have to be shipped to Ethiopia — the very country where Toby's compassion for the beggar boy had moved him to act.[2]

How many times have you felt compassion only to make up your mind that acting on it is impossible? Think again. Why couldn't God give you an experience like Toby's? If He can work this way through the compassionate willingness of a high school student, how much more can He supernaturally orchestrate the logistics in your reality?

WHEN TO BAIL

Lisa pushed open our church doors one fine spring morning and turned heads immediately. From her magnificent hair to her red business suit and matching accessories to her three-inch heels, she looked like a fashion plate.

In addition to her stunning appearance, this corporate queen possessed phenomenal people skills reflecting a surprising degree of down-to-earth vulnerability. Lisa charmed us overnight, and soon she and her family had blended into the deeper levels of our church life through small-group ministry involvement.

Because Lisa and her family hailed from a church nearby, we contacted their former pastor as a matter of course to find out why he thought they had left. He sighed and probably thirsted for a glass of water to rinse the sour taste from his mouth.

"Difficult," he answered politely. Though he had attempted mediation and reconciliation, these folks seemed to stir up trouble for sport. He hesitated when we invited him to join us in talking with them about our potential concerns. Though willing to meet, he recommended including a trained counselor.

When we approached Lisa and her family about clearing the air with their previous church in order to get off to a better start with us, the idea went over like a lead balloon.

Yet they continued worshiping with us without incident — for a while.

During this calm before the storm, we learned more about Lisa's damaged childhood. That helped explain her mercurial behavior, especially directed toward her husband. He landed in the hospital at her hands more than once. The hot-tempered fits she displayed against him soon jumped like electricity to others. No wonder a growing group at church stopped returning her phone calls. Some invested in better home security systems instead.

Lisa took their rejection personally. How could good church people distance themselves from her? Why would they not accept her? In time, she targeted Eric and me.

Counseling professionals say that hurting people hurt people. Keep that in mind when you reach out with compassion. Just as God's love spills out of emotionally healthy believers filled with His spirit, unrepentant wounded folks often spill what's inside too. Living with the "spillage" can be difficult at best.

Lisa was no exception. To her credit, she knew she needed meaningful relationships. But her brokenness stripped away any possibility of forming those relationships. She absolutely refused to visit a counselor to help her win the war raging inside — and out.

For one thing, she feared psychological testing, and every counselor she visited required testing to get a baseline reading on her. We skipped formal evaluation but insisted on meeting Lisa and her husband privately. Lisa pouted and pointed out that she wanted people to accept her — period. Her attitude proved maddening. Besides resisting an honest look at herself, she denied any responsibility for the relational chaos now ricocheting around our church.

The family finally fled after draining us to our last drop of energy, and it took months and many conversations to debrief our faith community. Amazingly, this one very wounded person created an epidemic insecurity about how we individually and corporately should show compassion.

Reflecting on the nasty backlash of that relationship saddens me because it shows that we couldn't effectively reach into Lisa's world with God's love. We tried to speak truth against the lies she believed about herself and others, but she persistently rejected that truth. At some point, we decided to bail. Even in your commitment to live with a patchwork heart, you will occasionally reach the same painful impasse with someone you are trying to help.

God may call you to show compassion to a stranger — no strings attached. However, if you've given Him *carte blanche* availability in the ministry of compassion, expect more extended contact. Unlike broken bones, which heal relatively quickly, bruised spirits and emotions usually take months or even years to heal. Making a new friend involves being prepared to journey with her through many transitions — sometimes slowly and painfully.

It's tough to know when and where to draw the healthiest boundaries. This is especially confounding since I understand compassion as a characteristic intended to expand my heart, not protect it. Yet, the question remains. When is it time to bail? How long do you stay in a relationship based on compassion when inappropriate behavior like Lisa's continues?

In the Sermon on the Mount Jesus taught the disciples to lay aside judgment in favor of love — specifically for their enemies (Matthew 5:43-48). But later He stated: "Do not give dogs what is sacred; do not throw your pearls to pigs. If you do, they may trample them under their feet, and then turn and tear you to pieces" (7:6).

Why did Jesus issue this warning in the middle of what seems to be love-fest teaching? He knew the value of His work on the cross. He didn't take that work lightly, and neither should we. The fully human Jesus understood that this world is home to both givers and takers. Takers don't often discern how much they take. They scavenge for anything they can get from whomever they can get it.

Givers, on the other hand, don't often discern how much they give to these types. Jesus recognized the devastating potential of such teeter-totter dynamics — in both secular and sacred environments. For instance, there are Christian carpetbaggers who go fundraising from church to church, playing on the compassion of well-meaning believers. Then, they take the money and run! These taker-types prey on the compassion of others for emotional support as well.

Ultimately, knowing the difference requires both God-given discernment and "on-the-job" training. I have made many mistakes in my ministry of compassion. But I have learned how to establish better boundaries from those mistakes. To maintain a healthier perspective, remember several things.

Be a Friend, Not a Savior

Fifteen years ago, I thought my purpose on earth involved solving everyone's problems. Then, while listening to a radio program one afternoon while my children napped, I heard the term "Messiah complex" for the first time. The Christian counselor on the air explained that those afflicted with this complex feel a very distinct "calling" to right the wrongs in their world. This person — often a perfectionist — freely dispenses simple counsel to complex issues, whether or not others show the desire for advice.

I started biting my nails as my life flashed before me. Many scenes confirmed my Messianic tendencies. Instead of being a friend, I unwittingly had stepped into the role of savior. Many of these relationships headed south when the person upon whom I felt compassion simply resented my "help." Looking back, I now see I had tried to help too much. I was on a self-proclaimed mission to save the world!

The only problem is, I can't save the world and neither can you. Mere mortals don't have the power or authority to transform even one burned emotion or hurting cell in anyone's life. Our mission is more like a traffic cop's. We point people to the main event — Christ and His saving work on the cross. Besides, assuming the role of "Great Answer Giver" only causes people to stumble as they mistakenly put their hope in you rather than in God.

When I counsel hurting people, they usually want to know what I think about their situation. Then I ask them if they would like to know God's thoughts on the topic, and together we turn pages in the Bible before continuing the discussion. This accomplishes two purposes. One, it helps people realize that they can find God's answers for themselves by opening God's Word. Two, it changes their expectation about my role. Spoon-feeding them truth won't help them get stronger.

Finally, remember to resist the temptation to climb up on a pedestal — especially if some vulnerable person is more than willing to leave you there. Compassion isn't about feeling better about yourself. It's about obediently walking in Christ's footsteps. A self-centered motivation guarantees a dead-end experience because, sooner or later, you will feel underappreciated.

Be a Model, Not a Maid

Give a man a fish and he can eat for a day. Teach a man to fish and he will never be hungry again. How true! Yet I often fight the pressure to "do something" in order to truly help another. That response reminds me of a parent trying to help a child color a class project. It's easy to go overboard! But Jesus calls us to model His love, not to scurry around picking up the pieces of someone's broken life.

Recently, one of the women I counsel confessed that she had returned to her substance of choice during a weak moment. I couldn't believe that she hadn't tossed it in the garbage yet, especially in this fragile phase of her recovery.

"Do you want your life to be defined by your addiction?" I asked, looking her square in the eye. She emphatically objected and promised to clean house immediately.

At that juncture, I chose to be a model, not a maid. I lived a substance-free life and challenged her to the same. I could have dropped everything, run over to her house, and dramatically disposed of that substance to protect her from another binge. However, cleaning up after her would never be as effective as encouraging her to do the deed with her own two hands. That's part of her healing process. Every time she chooses to stop abusing that substance, she gets stronger.

Be Lovingly Confrontive, Not a Pushover

Remember that compassion often involves both comforting *and* lovingly confronting. I suspect many people become pushovers in the process of showing compassion. But is it compassionate or loving to allow people to walk all over you?

If you leave conversations with needy people feeling frustrated and stifled in expressing your point of view, stop and evaluate your own emotions and motivations. Why are you afraid to speak your mind? Why is it difficult to tell someone something you know she doesn't want to hear? You may be a closet pushover who needs to more directly confront the problematic issues and outline clearer boundaries.

Giving away pieces of your heart without proper boundaries is like doing trapeze work without a net. The chances of disaster are greater!

Needy people are just that — needy. If you're not careful, they will take over your life. So, Eric and I establish firm boundaries with these folks up front. We clearly explain that certain days are off limits to them because we reserve that time for our marriage and family. If a crisis crops up on a Sunday night, I usually wait until Monday morning to respond, unless it is an absolute emergency. What constitutes an emergency? If I think the person is suicidal, most definitely I would call back immediately. If there has been a death in the family or an unexpected hospitalization, I would make sure that someone contacts the person if I were unable to do it.

Besides giving me time with Eric and the kids, boundaries give me time to myself. This is no luxury. Rather, it's a critical weekly preparation if you plan on showing compassion to hurting people over the long haul. Allowing them free access to your life is not the way to go. It's unhealthy and draining, and it will burn you like a moth caught in a bug zapper.

A person who is journeying well through her pain will respect your boundaries and respond, however slowly, to God's truth in her situation. If she cannot respect time or other boundaries, rehashes the same conversation without changing, or resists healing alternatives — it may be time to bail.

Letting go represents a last-resort boundary to protect you from a shameless taker. Naturally, given the vulnerability of needy people, how you end the relationship matters much. The apostle Paul calls believers to the ministry of reconciliation (2 Corinthians 5:19). Love and a spirit of reconciliation should lace your thoughts and words if this kind of exit conversation becomes necessary. I also recommend asking your pastor or spiritual mentor to join you to help mediate the conversation and bring additional spiritual insight.

Chapter Ten

It's Not Always Time to Bail

After reading about characters like Lisa and when to bail, you suddenly may be reconsidering everything you've read in this book. But I want to encourage you that the rewards of a patchwork heart far outweigh the pain. For every Lisa, there are probably ten or more Jennifers.

In April of 2001, I flew to Hungary to meet a team launched by Art2Hearts, the nonprofit organization I direct that arranges cross-cultural learning experiences for artists to creatively share the gospel. That year, Jennifer led the team to Hungary.

Just before I left the United States, Jen e-mailed a note to update me on the team's progress to date. Her words practically danced off my computer screen. While reading her joyful description of events, I couldn't help but remember when I first met Jen and how she had grown since then.

Jennifer had shown up at our church one Sunday during her junior year in college. She had met Eric at the college after enrolling in his drama class, and got to know him better through participating on the school's traveling drama team. Because of her off-the-charts energy and excellent work ethic, Eric soon asked her to help him coordinate the drama team's comings and goings.

Later, when Jen casually offered to help me book dates for my concert ministry, my thoughts took wing. I could really use her organizational skills and upbeat attitude. But while she brought much-needed gifts to my office, she brought baggage too. Everyone has some sort of baggage, and for Jen high-pressure situations invariably lit her short fuse. Her temper flared whenever the equipment malfunctioned or if there were transportation delays or schedule changes. Things would be tense for a few days, and she typically withdrew to the safety of her apartment (or to her motel room, if she was traveling with me) to cry and nurse her emotional wounds. This hampered our productivity and concerned me as well. At last I confronted her and braced myself for the backlash.

That's when Jen took me off guard. She told me that she was aware of her problem and willing to work on it. Unlike Lisa, Jen brought humility and a teachable spirit to our relationship. That's when my kernel of compassion for her started to sprout.

Many conversations later, when I had taken the time to understand the source of Jen's rage, my heart softened more. After all, she had grown up as the only girl and the baby of a family with three brothers — and eventually three fathers too. Her half-brothers joined the family through her mom's first marriage. The second marriage produced Jen.

Jen's mother recently accepted Christ and now serves as an intercessory prayer warrior for many ministries, including our own. But before making this life-changing decision, she married the same type of guy three times — unstable and unpredictable. Her mother's divorces and partying lifestyle wreaked havoc on Jen's young life. She feared for her mother's life, her brothers' lives, and for her own. She feared abandonment. Over time, her terror hardened to anger and bursts of caustic behavior.

The turning point came when kindly neighbors befriended the nervous girl and took her to church. Jen met Jesus. She clung to Him during her parents' divorce and the jostling that ensued as they fought over custody. She later attended a Christian college in the Detroit area, and earned a degree in cross-cultural ministry. Seeing her use that degree on mission fields such as Hungary warms my heart.

Despite her faith and success, unresolved anger continued curdling her insides and periodically spewing out and burning others. During one of my weekend speaking engagements, Jen agreed to stay home to help manage the Sunday church service. When I later asked Eric about the service, he answered with one word. "Bumpy," he explained. Jen had gotten frazzled and lashed out at the team, which made for a tense Sunday morning.

Shortly thereafter, she cracked again under the pressure of rehearsing our Christmas musical. Instead of taking my stage direction, she argued so vehemently that I asked her to leave the room to regain her composure. That night, we parked in my driveway and sat uncomfortably in the car to discuss the fact that people and their feelings are more important than perfectionism. There's no reason to hurt others in the process of giving God excellence. We agreed on that perspective and, to maintain it in heated moments, we decided to start a new club — the "It's-not-a-big-deal" club.

When we struggled to polish our drama productions and music, she would jokingly say through clenched teeth, "It's not a big deal." But as we moved through the next year with this motto, I noticed a change in Jen — and so did others. Just as too many difficulties can cause a downward spiral, multiple goodnesses will most definitely cause an upward one. This was certainly true of Jen.

Our ministry was continuing to grow and opportunities seemed to be multiplying at a rapid rate. This was the good news that we had been praying for. In what should have been a joyous time, Jen came in one day and sat down heavily in her chair. I could tell something was wrong and I stopped long enough to give her the "So-what's-going-on?" glance. Sensing that I wasn't going to let her off the hook without an explanation, she asked for a moment to share something that was bothering her.

Her voice began to tremble and tears began to flow before she even spoke. "I have been keeping a secret for a while now. I don't want it to come out at a time when it could hurt what God is doing here. So I'm just going to tell on myself, and that way if anyone tries to accuse me, you'll already know about it."

I deeply appreciated her honesty and concern for me and the reputation of the ministry we cared for. I told her to open up the closet door and let the skeleton dance right out. There was certainly enough of God's grace to take care of it. She began to tell me about a relationship she had been involved in that had become sexually inappropriate. I let her finish telling the story, though I knew a great deal of it already because I knew the other person who had been involved.

"Jen, I knew about the unhealthy nature of your relationship before I hired you. But I also saw you taking drastic measures to get out of the relationship. In the years that you've been with me I've seen nothing that would make me doubt that you are living from a place of sexual purity. Undoubtedly you have sought God's forgiveness in regard to this, right?" She nodded that indeed she had. "Then that's good enough for me."

In the days that followed we had several more conversations that provided further healing and perspective on how that relationship had turned south. With each new understanding Jen became freer to embrace her identity in Christ, and something else happened too. She began to be *thankful* to the people who had helped her on her journey, and sought ways to contribute and give of her own life to others.

Today, I watch her as she interacts with artists. I hear her pray with passion for the salvation of the nations. I see her chasing my son Hunter around the house letting his silly giggling fill up the living room. And I realize each time that I am privileged to see a miracle of God in front of my very eyes. I watched Him transform Jen into the image of Christ and the beautiful dream He had for her life. I don't think I'll ever get over that, and I don't think I want to.

Don't let the takers of this world rob you of a priceless experience. Sure, there are those who would take you for a ride and waste your time and God's. But I know that He will help you steer clear of those aimless taking types and lead you right to the person whose life will be turned upside down by His love expressed through your patch-work heart.

Conclusion

COMPASSION'S LEGACY

What brings purpose to life? I get asked that a lot. Bottom line: loving God and loving people. Don't let the simplicity of that statement throw you off. What is very easily written is not as handily lived out. This we know. But what would happen to our world if today you chose to embrace this patchwork heart philosophy and began living it out? What would happen to the people whose lives brush up against yours — neighbors, teachers, grocery store clerks, coworkers, family, and friends? How would eternity be affected?

The richest and most rewarding part of life is not found in the things we possess — the house we live in or the car we drive. In this life, our greatest sense of fulfillment will always come from giving away our hearts for others and for the Savior. And in the life to come, what joy there will be in coming before our Maker with those whom we have loved in this life, and letting them stand as a testament to what love and grace can help us become.

I challenge you not to let the Evil One alter your course one inch as you set out on compassion's adventure. Learn what it means to be a grace-giver and live it out fully. Then be obedient when God calls and orchestrates divine appointments for you. Clothe yourself with love and turn your eyes and heart toward your world. There's no way to even imagine what God will do with hearts that are full of Him and willing to be given away.

BIBLE STUDY

Chapter 1

1. On a scale of one to ten, with one being no compassion and ten being high compassion, how do you rate and why?

2. What would you like God to do in your heart as a result of participating in this study?

3. Read Matthew 22:36-40. The essence of the Ten Commandments involves loving God and loving people. Are you relating to God and others with love? Why? Why not?

4. When you encounter someone who is especially needy, what is your knee-jerk reaction? Explain.

5. In *The Reflective Life,* Ken Gire writes:

Before we can love our neighbor, we must see our neighbor and hear our neighbor. Observing the way a gardener observes plants. Watching their buds when they're blooming. Watering their roots when they're wilting. But we cannot weep with those who weep or rejoice with those who rejoice unless we first see something of their tears or hear something of their laughter. If we can learn to see and hear our neighbor, maybe, just maybe, we can learn to see and hear

God. And seeing Him and hearing Him, to love Him. (p. 14)

List ways a gardener nurtures her patch. Then, list ways you can nurture a more vibrant relationship with God and others. Which of these relational principles proves most challenging? Why?

Gardening   *Relationships*

In Jeremiah 29:13 we learn that those who earnestly seek the Lord will find Him. If you will commit to earnestly seek God in the area of loving others, He will have the freedom to reshape your heart. Take some time now to read through the Compassion Covenant and Prayer. If you are willing to embark on compassion's journey, sign the covenant below.

Prayer:
Loving Father,

I find myself at a crossroads once again in my walk with You. Having experienced Your leading in my life before, I realize that there are now new heights that await me if I will simply follow Your lead. My heart wants to see and experience what those mountaintops hold for me. I also realize that there will be valleys to cross in this journey, and for those I need Your grace, courage, and perseverance.

I'm choosing to walk this path of loving others with You. Your Word tells me that You will never forsake me or leave me alone, and that it will guide my way. I believe that is true and trust Your promises. Be with me on this new path. Help me to understand myself better as I learn how to love at a deeper level from the One who loves me unconditionally and deeply.

Help me to be a different and more loving person because of my time in Your Word and in Your presence. Like Samuel, I say to you, "Speak Lord, for your servant listens." In Jesus' name,
Amen.

Covenant:

Today I welcome the opportunity to come into accountability to God and those who study this book with me in the area of loving others. I understand the need to be honest in my answers and discussion so that God may bring to the surface those things in my life that need to be reshaped so that I can love others freely and well. To the best of my ability I will obey the Spirit's leading in my life and share my growth steps with my trusted friends in this study so that we might encourage each other and build each other up. I will commit to doing the lessons each week, even the ones that are personally difficult for me, allowing God the opportunity to work in my heart through life's hard moments. I acknowledge my complete dependency on God for life change and transformation and hold on to His promise that He will complete the work He has begun in me.

Signed: _____

Date: _____

Chapter 2

1. In the movie *Shadowlands*, loving and losing Joy reshapes C. S. Lewis's heart. What experiences have caused you to change how you love others? Explain.

2. When pain presents itself, do you usually turn to God, to others, or to yourself for comfort?

3. Read James 1 in your Bible. Then, reread the excerpt of this passage from *The Message* as printed in chapter 2, p. 31. Both versions call believers to view pain as a positive agent of inner change. What can you do to cooperate in this process?

4. Instead of facing pain, sometimes it seems easier to cope with life by seeking temporary relief in shopping, eating, decorating, reading novels, overworking, over-sleeping, hiding out, or thrill seeking. What coping mechanisms could you drop to let God work more effectively through your pain?

5. If you rejected quick-fix comforts, how could God comfort you instead?

6. Read 2 Corinthians 1:2-7 and Philippians 3:10. How do these verses impact your perspective on suffering?

7. Preparing yourself *before* pain strikes will help you cope better when it does. Brainstorm with others in the group to devise a Christ-centered pain management plan.

Prayer:

Heavenly Father,

I acknowledge that repentance is an important part of Your transformational plan in my life. It begins when I turn away from my old ways and toward Your ways. I realize that I have often chosen to anesthetize my pain rather than to seek You when I am hurting. Today, I choose to change. I choose You. Please be my comfort and prompt me by Your Spirit when I am tempted to return to my old patterns of coping. I accept Your comfort and turn from counterfeits. Amen.

Chapter 3

1. Kim begins this chapter with a story of when she felt like an outsider.

    a. Have you ever been excluded?

    b. What did it feel like?

    c. In retrospect, how would someone's compassionate response have helped you? Why?

2. Jesus listened carefully to His Father's heart when He ministered. As a result, He saw needy people through God's eyes and responded with compassion. Note Jesus' actions in each of these verses. What did He do that helped Him see what God saw?

a. Matthew 14:22-23

b. Mark 1:35

c. John 14:31

3. Read John 15:3-4,10-12; Romans 12:1-2; Ephesians 4:22; and Colossians 3:12. Practically speaking, how can you allow God to clothe you with compassion (*oiktirmos*) so you can exhibit compassion (*splanchnon*) to others?

4. After reading chapter 3, whom would you nominate for compassion's hall of fame? Why?

5. Who in your life would benefit if you responded to him or her with more compassion?

Prayer:

Thank You for moving my heart toward the things that matter to You, Lord. I confess that many times I fail to pause and see the needs You see in the people around me. Forgive me for being so self-absorbed that I miss what Your heart wants me to know. Help me to see _____ the way You see her or him. Help me to extend myself as You lead. I humbly rely on You now to show me how to offer a sincere expression of Your love. Amen.

Chapter 4

1. To show compassion over the long haul, it helps to come from a place of inner peace and calm each day. Take a step back and look at your life. Would you say that overall your life is highly charged (full steam ahead) or calm (tuned in)?

2. In *Hearing God,* Dallas Willard asserts that God wants to speak to each of us in a very personal way. Does that sound novel or "normal" to you? Why?

3. Look at John 10:27. This text describes Jesus as a Shepherd and His followers as sheep. Because of all the time the sheep spend with the Shepherd, they easily recognize and trust His voice. How recognizable is God's voice to you?

4. Are you content with your spiritual listening skills?

5. Has God ever spoken to you specifically and power-fully? How did you respond?

6. It is easy to approach our prayer times with a list of things to talk about. Prayer is more aptly described as a conversation with God.

   a. Are your prayers more often monologues or dia-logues?

b. Do you listen to God as much as you talk to Him?

c. Is it difficult to pray? Why?

7. Dallas Willard suggests that some go deaf to God's voice because they don't want to follow His will. The children of Israel were notoriously deaf when it came to listening to God — sometimes so are we! Read Isaiah 5:24. Have there been times when you turned a deaf ear to God because you didn't want to hear Him?

8. This week, give God the opportunity to speak as you study and meditate on the verses below. Wait silently and make notes in your study guide about His responses. Note: Resist getting frustrated if you don't receive an immediate response. Instead, keep your heart open to Him all day — He often shows up unexpectedly!

Monday: Luke 10:38-42

Tuesday: Ephesians 1:17-21

Wednesday: John 14:21-23

Thursday: John 15:16

Friday: Matthew 11:29

Saturday: 1 Corinthians 1:27-29

Sunday: Romans 8:15-16

Prayer:

Heavenly Father,

I must confess that I haven't been listening much to You recently. Sometimes it's easier to just talk to You, rather than sitting in the silence and listening for Your voice. But I am making a choice today to change the way I communicate with You so that You can say the things that are on Your heart.

Forgive me for the times I turned a deaf ear to You on purpose because I knew what You were going to say and I just didn't want to do it. Will you give me Your grace and strength so that I may be more courageous in following You? My desire is to know Your voice and respond to Your call.

In Jesus' name,

Amen.

Chapter 5

1. When Kim refused to befriend the woman she met in the park, she suffered a crisis in obedience. Have you experienced anything similar? Explain.

2. John Calvin wrote: "True knowledge of God is born out of obedience." Is this true in your relationship with God? Explain.

3. Read John 8:31. Compare it to 1 John 3:21-24 and John 14:23-24. What role does obedience play in understanding freedom and truth?

4. In Isaiah 20:2, God commands the prophet to take off his clothes and his sandals as a sign of judgment against two of Israel's enemies. Has God ever asked you to do something particularly unusual, difficult, or humbling? What influenced your decision to obey or disobey?

5. First Samuel 17:41-50 and Joshua 2:3-15 describe other cases of radical obedience. How did these biblical characters respond?

6. First Samuel 15:22 confirms God's delight in obedience. In which areas do you obey well? Which areas need work?

Prayer:

Once again, Lord, shine the light of Your truth in my heart and reveal any area of disobedience. I choose today to believe that You long for my obedience. I will depend on You for the strength to obey. Amen.

Chapter 6

1. What are your top two compassion squelchers? Explain.

2. Luke 10:30-37 recounts the story of the Good Samaritan. Why do some choose to turn from needy people? (See Matthew 23:23-24.)

3. Fear represents one of the heaviest compassion squelchers. Looking inside your heart, what would you say is your greatest compassion-busting fear? Look up the following verses to find how God views fear:

Psalm 56:3

2 Timothy 1:7

1 John 4:18

4. Time constraints squelch compassion as well. How would you describe your current schedule?

❏ You keep your planner by the bed with a night-light; you're thinking of installing a revolving door on the house for faster take-off and land-ing; people are happy if you show up, but you're always late.

❏ You're learning to say "no" but it still makes you sweat; sometimes you regret moving the planner off the bedside table; you consistently run ten minutes late.

❏ "No" is becoming easier all the time; you noticed the birds singing this morning and realized for the first time that birds live on your street; you're arriving on schedule most of the time.

❑ You took a walk last week just for the fun of being outdoors — it felt weird at first, but you scheduled one for next week too; you're always on time and sometimes you even arrive early.

❑ Life has its busy seasons, ups and downs, but the pace is not frenetic; you regularly do things you enjoy, including walks; you consistently arrive early with enough time to stop for coffee.

5. Based on your schedule, do you have enough time to love God and love others? If not, what can you change? Make a list of your responsibilities and activities. This week, ask the Holy Spirit to show you what to get rid of and what to let go.

6. Do you like to be in control? To love others well with compassion, you must relinquish control and give God the freedom to move you past your favorite squelchers. Does that make you nervous? Why? Why not?

7. Read Hosea 11:3-4; Romans 8:38-39; Ephesians 2:4-5; 3:17-19; and 1 John 3:1. How do these verses affect the amount of control you give God?

8. Read Galatians 3:26-29. How does God view prejudice? What things make you most intolerant of others?

9. Read Matthew 28:19-20. List three to five action steps that would help you overcome your complacency.

Prayer:

Dear Lord,

I acknowledge the many compassion squelchers Satan uses to keep me from following Christ's example. Please help me overcome my top three squelchers. I choose today to empty myself of these in favor of You filling me with Your compassion. Amen.

Chapter 7

1. Does a faith adventure sound fascinating or frightening? Why?

2. Read this translation of Hebrews 11:7:

   By faith, Noah built a ship in the middle of dry land. He was warned about something he couldn't see, and acted on what he was told. The result? His family was saved. His act of faith drew a sharp line between the evil of the unbelieving world and the rightness of the believing world. As a result, Noah became intimate with God. (MSG)

   Noah's contemporaries thought he was crazy. Yet, he believed God more than them. Have family or friends ever questioned a faith step you took? How did you respond? Did their questions cause you to doubt God or trust Him more?

3. According to Hebrews 11, faith involves believing that God can accomplish whatever He wants — even when a situation seems impossible. When you recognize a new faith adventure, how will you proceed? Can you, by faith, let God be God in the midst of your adventure?

4. When we are afraid to let God be Himself in our lives, we keep ourselves at a safe distance from Him by placing Him in a box whose boundaries we define. For instance, *I can't go on that missions trip because I'm not a good traveler,* or *I could never raise the necessary funds. I can't teach that weight management class at church because I'm not sure I'm a teacher. I can't start this ministry because I've never led anything before.* Describe the box into which you may have placed God.

5. Second Corinthians 1:20-21 states that all of God's promises are available because of Christ's finished work on the cross. How does that change your attitude toward faith adventures?

6. Is there currently a situation in your life that seems beyond the scope of your compassion? Why?

7. What does God promise to do in the midst of such "impossible" situations? (Use your concordance and ask your Bible study leader or pastor for help if you get stuck.)

Prayer:

Strong and Loving Father,

I admit I have kept a safe distance from You out of fear and lack of trust. I'm seeing now the unlimited possibilities that lie ahead for me if I will choose to trust You and allow You to work Your dreams in my life. If I am to love well the people You have given me to love, I must be willing to entertain the idea that You will call me to some impossible situations so that Your power and glory can be displayed. I choose that pathway today and ask You to teach me what it means to really trust You fully and completely.

Help me, loving Father, to embrace faith in ways I have not before. I look with great anticipation into the future to see the fulfillment of Your promises in my life.

In the strong and mighty name of Jesus,

Amen.

Chapter 8

1. One quality of a grace-giver is the willingness to live with the pain of relating to others. Kim shared the story of her friend Jackie and how the pain in that early friendship caused her to be cautious and less trusting. Could you relate? Have there been people in your life who have, through their words and actions, caused you to be careful in the way you reach out in friendship?

2. What do you find yourself doing to insulate your feelings against the pain of giving in your relationships?

3. Honesty is a key to authentic grace-giving. John 15:5 and James 4:6 highlight God's view of honesty. Jot down what you see as the important thrust of each verse.

   a. Are there ways in which you think or act that need to come under the scrutiny of the truths of these verses?

   b. Is your life characterized by humility?

   c. Do you readily acknowledge your dependence on God?

4. Corrie ten Boom's confrontation with her former prison guard illustrates how God can help a willing person forgive — even in the most difficult situations. Look up 2 Corinthians 12:9. Have you found this to be true in your life? Explain.

5. Being forgiven encourages forgiveness. Have you ever been forgiven by a person you deeply hurt? How did this affect you?

6. Patience is another key ingredient to authentic grace-giving. Are you a patient person? Why? Why not?

7. In *Compassion*, Henri Nouwen explains that patience must be a central part of your life if you want to love well. Is this a difficult teaching? Why? Why not?

8. Colossians 3:12 calls believers to clothe themselves with compassion. How does that happen? (See Romans 5:1-5.)

9. Becoming a compassionate grace-giver involves embracing forgiveness, honesty, and patience. Which one most often holds you back?

Prayer:

Dear Father,

I understand that to love others the way You love them, I must allow You to transform my heart and mind. Help me overcome the things that stifle my grace-giving. Apart from You I can do nothing, but with You all things are possible. Amen.

Chapter 9

1. When you hear a story like Christina's do you:

   a. Think those kinds of incredible stories only happen to other people?

   b. Hope that life never gets that exciting for you?

   c. Wonder if God wants to write a chapter like Christina's in your life?

2. Read Psalm 84:11. What does God promise if you obey Him?

3. Read Job 42:1-2. Does God want to communicate His plans to you? What causes you to doubt that? (See James 1:5-8.)

4. If you choose to live a life of compassion, you must be willing to let God reorder your days. When God abruptly sends you in a different direction, do you feel frustrated or excited? Why?

5. What mental and emotional adjustments would make you more flexible?

6. Toby's story reminds us that if God wants something to happen, it will happen. Has there ever been a time in your life when God asked you to do something you thought was humanly impossible? What was your response? What was the outcome?

7. Does the thought of embracing impossibility make you nervous or anxious? Why? Why not?

8. It is human nature to take on God's part of an endeavor. We look at a task and automatically begin to figure out how we can do it. Read 1 Thessalonians 5:23-24 and Matthew 19:26. What do they teach about your job and God's job in terms of responding to challenging situations?

Prayer:

Father God,

I acknowledge that when I ask You to give me compassion, You will show me what to do with it. I trust You to give me flexibility, strength, and hope. Help me to trust You in new ways so that You can orchestrate the events of my life to glorify Your name. Amen.

Chapter 10

1. What are appropriate limits or boundaries when dealing with difficult people? In Matthew 7:6 Jesus discouraged His disciples from throwing pearls to pigs, another way of cautioning discernment. Is this a new concept for you? Explain.

2. Do you struggle to draw appropriate boundaries? Why? Why not?

3. Read 2 Corinthians 4:6-7 and Ephesians 4:2-6. Kim writes about being a friend, not a savior. How do these verses help you clarify the difference?

4. Read Colossians 4:6 and Ephesians 4:14-15,22-25. What do these verses teach about relating to others as a truth-teller?

5. What mental and emotional roadblocks keep you from being a truth-teller? How can God help you overcome them?

6. If you choose to live a more active life of compassion, which boundaries may challenge you the most?

   ❑ Spending too much time with the needy person.

   ❑ Trying to rescue that person when he or she makes mistakes.

   ❑ Doing too much for him or her.

   ❑ Trying to solve his or her problems.

   ❑ Over-identifying with his or her needs.

   ❑ Troubleshooting his or her life.

7. Boundaries will protect you from burnout as well as from unnecessary frustration and hurt. As you establish boundaries around your ministry of compassion, discuss those plans with your pastor, Bible study leader, friends, and family. Ask them to hold you accountable. List below three people that you would ask to hold you accountable. Make an appointment with them in the next three weeks to discuss with them what you are learning and how they can help you begin to reach out in a healthy way through appropriate boundaries.

Prayer:

Father,

I confess that I have allowed fear and inappropriate boundaries to hinder my ministry of compassion. I choose today to follow Your example of compassion. Instead of being a pushover, I want to more freely comfort and lovingly confront when necessary. I welcome Your Spirit to show me where my boundaries are in order to love others well without losing myself in the process. Amen.

NOTES

Chapter One

1. Bruce Bugbee and Don Cousins, *Network Participant's Guide* (Grand Rapids, Mich.: Zondervan, 1994), p. 43.
2. Ken Gire, *The Reflective Life* (Colorado Springs: Chariot Victor, 1998), p. 77.

Chapter Two

1. Oswald Chambers, *My Utmost for His Highest* (Uhrichsville, Ohio: Barbour Publishing, 1997), p. 286.

Chapter Three

1. W. E. Vine, *Vine's Expository Dictionary of New Testament Words* (McLean, Va.: MacDonald Publishing Company [no year listed], p. 220.
2. Edward LeJoly and Jaya Chaliha, *Reaching Out in Love* (New York: Continuum Publishing Company, 2000), p. 25.

Chapter Four

1. Dallas Willard, *Hearing God* (Downers Grove, Ill.: InterVarsity, 1999), p. 22.
2. Howard Macy, *Rhythms of the Inner Life* (Old Tappan, N. J.: Revell, 1988), p. 51.
3. Mother Teresa of Calcutta, *A Simple Faith,* (New York: Random House, 1995), p. 7.

4. Jill Briscoe, *Prayer That Works* (Wheaton, Ill.: Tyndale, 2000), p. 111.
5. Dallas Willard, *Hearing God*, p. 71.
6. Jill Briscoe, *Prayer That Works*, p. 19.

Chapter Five

1. Quoted in Eugene H. Petersen, *A Long Obedience in the Same Direction* (Downers Grove, Ill.: InterVarsity, 2000).
2. David Nasser, *A Call to Die* (Baxter Press, 2000), p. 281.
3. Jill Briscoe, *Prayer That Works* (Wheaton, Ill.: Tyndale, 2000), p. 56.
4. Neil T. Anderson, *The Bondage Breaker* (Eugene, Oreg: Harvest House, 1997), p. 248.
5. Alan Redpath, *Victorious Christian Living*, (Out of Print).
6. Oswald Chambers, *My Utmost for His Highest* (Uhrichsville, Ohio: Barbour Publishing, 1997), p. 271.

Chapter Seven

1. Ken Gire, *Moments with the Savior* (Grand Rapids, Mich.: Zondervan, 1998), p. 195.
2. Ken Gire, *Moments with the Savior*, pp. 203-204.
3. Eugene H. Peterson, *A Long Obedience in the Same Direction* (Downers Grove, Ill.: InterVarsity, 2000), p. 17.
4. Eugene H. Peterson, *A Long Obedience in the Same Direction*, p. 79.
5. Frederick Buechner, *A Room Called Remember* (San Francisco: HarperSanFrancisco, 1992), pp. 20-21.
6. Eugene H. Peterson, *A Long Obedience in the Same Direction*, p. 90.

Chapter Eight

1. Corrie ten Boom, *Tramp for the Lord* (Old Tappan, N.J.: Revell, 1974), pp. 55-57.
2. Henri J. M. Nouwen, *Compassion: A Reflection on the Christian Life* (New York: Image Books, Doubleday, 1982), p. 92.
3. Henri J. M. Nouwen, *Compassion: A Reflection on the Christian Life,* p. 90.

Chapter Nine

1. Christina DiStefano Davis, *Totally Surrounded* (Seattle: YWAM Publishing, 2000), p. 14.
2. John Ortberg, *If You Want to Walk on Water, You Have to Get Out of the Boat* (Grand Rapids, Mich.: Zondervan, 2000), p. 89.

Kim Moore

KIM MOORE is on the teaching staff of Speak Up with Confidence seminars, a Christian communicators' seminar that is taught by Carol Kent. As a speaker, vocal artist, and worship leader, Kim has been traveling the U.S. and abroad for twelve years.

A heart for missions has permeated Kim's ministry from the start, and in the year 2000, Kim Moore Ministries formed Art2Hearts International Ministries. Art2Hearts links artists (musical, vocal, visual, and dramatic) with mission opportunities around the world.

Kim and her husband, Eric, live in Plymouth, Michigan, with their three children, Lincoln, Brittany, and Hunter, and one loveable Wheaton terrier, Kaylee.

Pam Mellskog

PAM MELLSKOG lives in Boulder, Colorado — home of the stately Flatiron mountain range and an amazing macramé necklace and tie-dye T-shirt trade. In this panoramic setting populated by some of the country's most eclectic folks, she enjoys people-watching, hiking, biking, and riding a midnight-black Tennessee walker named Velvet.

As if freelance writing wasn't enough of an adventure, Pam plunged into leading the junior high group at her church in 2000. She has recruited several of the most hyper members to help her update her recent home purchase with its crazy circa 1970 kitchen décor (burnt-orange countertops, a marigold-colored stove, funky cabinetry, fixtures, and linoleum with a French floret-looking pattern in avocado, mustard, and brown shades). She thanks them for their compassion.

OTHER WARM, REFLECTIVE BOOKS FOR WOMEN.

The Allure of Hope

Hope holds out the alluring promise of good to come. But it also carries risks. *The Allure of Hope* will help you keep an open, hopeful heart even in the face of deep disappointment or loss.
(Jan Meyers)

Detours, Tow Trucks, and Angels in Disguise

Sometimes God is found where you least expect Him to be. Filled with true-to-life stories, this book will make you laugh and cry as you see God at work in your life.
(Carol Kent)

Deceived by Shame, Desired by God

Learn how the healing love of God can bring good out of your darkest, most shameful secrets.
(Cynthia Spell Humbert)

To get your copies, visit your local bookstore, call 1-800-366-7788, or log on to www.navpress.com. Ask for a FREE catalog of NavPress products. Offer #BPA.

NAVPRESS

BRINGING TRUTH TO LIFE
www.navpress.com

90464